.

The Washington, DC Media Corps in the 21st Century

The Washington, DC Media Corps in the 21st Century

The Source-Correspondent Relationship

Lea Hellmueller

palgrave
macmillan

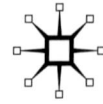

THE WASHINGTON, DC MEDIA CORPS IN THE 21ST CENTURY
Copyright © Lea Hellmueller, 2014.

First published in 2014 by
PALGRAVE MACMILLAN®
in the United States—a division of St. Martin's Press LLC,
175 Fifth Avenue, New York, NY 10010.

Where this book is distributed in the UK, Europe and the rest of the world,
this is by Palgrave Macmillan, a division of Macmillan Publishers Limited,
registered in England, company number 785998, of Houndmills,
Basingstoke, Hampshire RG21 6XS.

Palgrave Macmillan is the global academic imprint of the above companies
and has companies and representatives throughout the world.

Palgrave® and Macmillan® are registered trademarks in the United States,
the United Kingdom, Europe and other countries.

ISBN: 978–1–137–39859–8

Library of Congress Cataloging-in-Publication Data

Hellmueller, Lea.
    The Washington, DC media corps in the 21st century : the
source-correspondent relationship / by Lea Hellmueller.
        pages cm
    Includes bibliographical references and index.
    ISBN 978–1–137–39859–8 (alk. paper)
        1. Journalism—Political aspects—Washington (DC)—History—
21st century. 2. Journalism—Objectivity—Washington (DC)—History—
21st century. 3. Reporters and reporting—Washington (DC)—History—
21st century. 4. Foreign correspondents—Washington (D.C.)—History—
21st century. 5. Confidential communications—Press—Washington (D.C.)
I. Title.

PN4899.W29H46 2014
071'.3—dc23   2014003484

A catalogue record of the book is available from the British Library.

Design by Newgen Knowledge Works (P) Ltd., Chennai, India.

First edition: July 2014

Contents

Figures

Tables

Acknowledgments

Long Beach, CA; Fribourg, Switzerland; Santa Clara, CA; Stanford, CA; Columbia, MO; Washington, DC—this dissertation carries the imprint of places related to people who not only encouraged my work but also shaped it with their ideas and guidance in those cities.

What started with a small idea in Switzerland turned into a long and exciting journey. I'm particularly thankful for having had the unique opportunity to work with and learn from the gatekeeping expert, Prof. Tim P. Vos. He coached me through research challenges with his sharp mind and great humor, and he encouraged me to think of questions that I had never thought of before. I am thankful for his willingness to share his cultural capital and his constant mentoring by taking the time to narrow down chaotic ideas into serious research designs. He opened my eyes and ears to new possibilities and never gave up in trying to understand my writing.

As an undergraduate student, I had the privilege to study at California State University, Long Beach, where I met Prof. Lynda McCroskey. She became more than a mentor—a true friend who believed in my strength. She encouraged me to continue with graduate school at a time when all I could think of was to become a sub-Saharan African correspondent. I express my heartfelt gratitude to her endless inspiration in teaching me what it entails to be a responsible scholar.

In Fribourg, I have been fortunate to work under the guidance of Prof. Louis Bosshart, whose teaching and mentoring style impressed me from the beginning. He supported my desire to study in the United States and provided assistance whenever I asked for help. He not only offered the resources and environment for scholarly development, but also enriched those experiences with research sabbaticals at Santa Clara University and Stanford University. Yosemite and Napa remain lively memories of times when hard work was interspersed with lovely distractions.

I am grateful for the funding that nourished the economic capital of what has become an exciting intellectual journey. In an early stage, it was the Fulbright program that enabled me to study and work at the world's first school of journalism, where I have been very fortunate to work with excellent faculty and critical thinkers. Later on, the Swiss NSF offered me another scholarship to extend my stay at the Missouri School of Journalism, which was enriched with dynamic debates in the classroom, in TV studios, and in research collaborations.

I express sincere thanks to all Washington, DC, correspondents, who were so crucial to this project. I could not have done it without them, and I was very fortunate that each of them showed a keen interest in my project. Without a doubt, access to their work and ideas provided the "meat" of this dissertation. This book testifies to the impact they had on my thinking about journalism in a multicultural and digital context. My very special thanks to Fernando Pizarro for his support with the data-gathering process and for engaging in in-depth discussion on DC journalism.

Moreover, thanks to my fellow PhD friends at Mizzou—especially You Li, Edson Tandoc, Saleem Alhabash, Erin Willis, Heather Shoenberger, Adam Maksl, Anna Kim, and Chad Painter. They supported my interest in conducting surveys, listened to my passionate speeches on field theory, fixed my computer, joined cooking contests, and provided a good relaxation from life in academia. I thank them for enhancing my social capital.

Very important to the writing part of this project was Youn-Joo Park, my grad-school friend and editor. Thanks for all your support and expertise you provided for my work.

Most important, my family—near and far—was crucial in emotionally supporting my academic path. I am more than proud to witness how much I learned from my sister whose commitment to work and passion for other cultures has greatly influenced my scholarly interests. My parents always encouraged me by claiming that "to lead the conversation is to ask questions." Questioning the status quo was the fuel, which drove my motivation to become a scholar. As Bourdieu (1990) wisely pointed out, "The progress of knowledge presupposes progress in knowledge of the conditions of knowledge."

Herzlichen Dank, merci beaucoup, and many thanks!

1
Introduction

I would rather go to jail than to give up a source. Sources are always important. They are everything.

—US correspondent, personal communication, Washington, DC, January 2012

Access to sources is the weather vane of journalistic success, and that is especially true in Washington, DC, where journalists cover one of the most politically powerful beats. Reliable sources in journalism are resources that build trust among audiences. Sources give meaning to an event, provide context and reasons, and a feeling of "being there" as they speak based on their own experiences and expertise. Trustworthy sources help establish the credibility of news stories and, in turn, of the news organization. While sources are important for journalists, the relationship journalists hold with key sources is also a delicate one, particularly in the capital where many journalists compete for the one sound bite and often keep their sources confidential.

Personal interviews and survey data collected for this book empirically examine how journalists' relationship with sources plays out in the 21st-century media landscape. While much has been written about how political power is established through the agenda setting of political issues, not much attention has been paid to social power, the form of getting politicians' voice heard through the relationship with journalists. Hence, the book maps out the delicate relationship between politicians and journalists from the perspective of US and foreign correspondents. This book analyzes the perception of correspondents about their relationships with DC politicians and their reporting strategies. In essence, the book reveals patterns of why sources get heard and how social power is established through building and maintaining close relationships with power holders. One political correspondent in DC revealed during an interview how strategic and complex relationships with politicians can be:

> A key White House staff member—he is dead, but I am leaving him nameless—had been a close friend at The University of Texas. I called on him one of my first days in town [Washington, DC], and he suggested that we take a walk. Outside, he said, in essence, "OK, I know you, and I trust you, and I will answer your questions when I can. But NEVER AGAIN call on me at the White House, either in person or by phone. If you have a question, call my home number and ask [my wife] to have me give you a call 'about the weekend.' You will probably not hear from me until 8 p.m. or so, when I can call you from home. But I will help you when I can, and if I can." He did just that. The spring of 1968, LBJ scheduled a long talk on Vietnam; the minute he opened his mouth, I filed a story with the Inquirer (written the previous day) with a lead that went something like this: "President Johnson stunned the nation Sunday night by announcing that he would neither seek nor accept nomination for re-election this year. (personal communication, Washington, DC, January 2012)

Source information is key to breaking a news story; important policy makers hold the power to know what will happen next and thus give journalists the material to inform their audiences about the future and consequences of important decision-making processes. Source materials enable journalists to carry out one of their main functions in society: to inform and to educate. Certainly, the power of sources over news is not news in itself: one of the most important examples involving the power of source materials is the Watergate scandal in 1972, in which the Nixon administration was discovered covering up its role in the break-in at the National Committee headquarters at the Watergate office. This scandal led to the resignation of President Nixon. The case bears an important place in the collective memory of journalism, as every detail of the investigation, from its fact checking to its organizational procedure, provides a role model of investigative reporting in DC. But more important is the strategic source use and source checking, which remains most often part of a side story rather than the main Watergate story. When journalist Bob Woodward was investigating on Watergate with his colleague Carl Bernstein, he came to conclusions based on information from sources, and the critical point was that Woodward's quoting a source was important for the breakthrough in the whole scandal (as he was using a secret information source named "Deep Throat"). Regarding the case, one of the correspondents remembered the following:

> And the managing editor came to Bob and he said to him, "I would like to speak to you. Who is your source?" And Bob said, "I cannot tell you, especially not in the newsroom." "Okay, fine; let's go." They walked from Fifteenth Street to McPherson Square and they were sitting down on a bench and made sure that no one was listening, including the FBI and others. He went with him and asked him: "Who is our source?" And it was the deputy director of the FBI. But the managing editor did his job. People trusted the source, because these two guys did their job very professionally. (personal communication, Washington, DC, January 2012)

The way journalists interact with sources has changed since the 1970s because of technological advances and professional knowledge of how to communicate more strategically with important policy makers. What remains the same is that sources have limited time and may provide exclusive information to one media organization at the expense of other journalists aiming to get an exclusive sound bite or interview. As prestigious source access is for journalists' own professional prestige, exclusive source material is still challenging for journalists to access, even though new communication channels such as social media provide enhanced opportunities to contact someone personally. Within that paradox, it is particularly important to point out that in the DC case, foreign correspondents struggle to gain access to important policy makers (Willnat and Weaver, 2003). Such lack of access to sources has become increasingly evident as the number of foreign correspondents in Washington, DC has increased over the past few decades; in 2008, the number was nearly 10 times what it was in 1968 when the US State Department first opened a foreign press center (Pew Research Center's Project for Excellence in Journalism, 2009; see figure 1.1). The increase in the number of foreign correspondents can be explained by international events that have led to an increased interest in US politics. For example, Al-Jazeera's English-language service opened a Washington bureau in 2006, and within three years of being in DC, the organization had already hired 86 staff members accredited to cover Congress in 2009 (Pew Research Center's Project for Excellence in Journalism, 2009).

In contrast to foreign media, the US mainstream media has reduced the number of staff in DC. However, this has led to a sharp growth

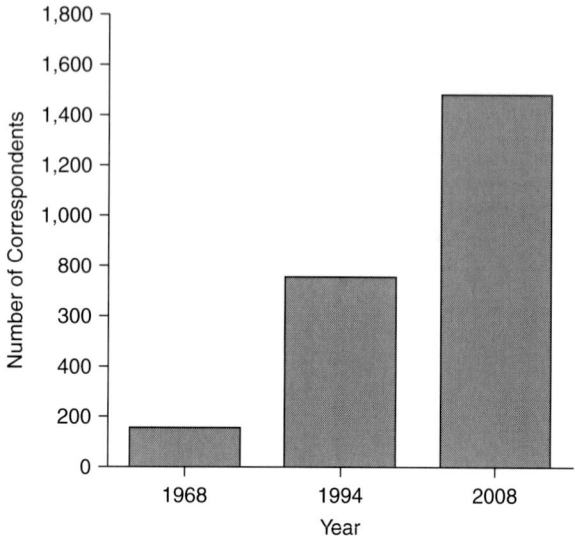

Figure 1.1   Foreign Correspondents Based in Washington, DC.
Source: Pew Research Center's Project for Excellence in Journalism, 2009.

among niche US media organizations and foreign media now represented in the capital, and DC has emerged as a transnational journalism news-gathering environment. That is, an increasing number of
journalists from around the globe, carrying with them their journalistic culture and native languages, compete for political sources in
DC and gather news alongside US journalists—traditional journalists, bloggers, or freelance staff. However, that is only one part of
the transnational journalism story. News organizations increasingly
target a transnational audience and thereby expand the audience
size. In fact, the launch of *Al-Jazeera America* in August 2013 is just
another example of how global media outlets headquartered in the
United States have become more global in their news-gathering routines by operating 70 offices overseas and approaching news content
as building global understanding. The same holds true for foreign
correspondence in the 21st century and for national news outlets targeting a culturally diverse audience within one country. For example,
Univision, a US-based news organization, provides content in Spanish
to more than 50 million Hispanics in the United States. There is no
doubt that globalization and increasing immigration have not only

intensified the need for such a network but they have also opened up new markets for targeting different ethnic groups within one country. National borders no longer reflect cultural borders or ethnic borders, as Reese (2001) has argued: "More important than national differences may be the emergence of a transnational global professionalism, the shape of which will greatly affect how well the world's press meets the normative standards we would wish for it" (p. 173).

The increase in foreign reporting alongside the emergence of transnational and global media outlets challenges long-believed standards in journalism; standards mostly learned and embraced within one country. News gathering in DC presents an environment where journalists from different countries come together and work at the same place. Because those journalists were mostly socialized to journalism practices in their native countries, they bring with them a variety of journalism cultures. Now, what happens if journalists work in a different environment than their home base? Does their "'journalism culture" change? And how do foreign correspondents affect the news culture in DC, if they have an impact at all? The idea in generating such questions is the fact that globalization has led to an interconnectedness of social systems; countries are no longer necessarily distinct but rather span national boundaries (de Mooij, 2010). Hence, the book contextualizes the relationship between correspondents and politicians based on criteria of transnational journalism culture explanations.

These research questions are important to consider because journalism culture is known to shape media content (Graber, 2002). Hence, the news-gathering environment in DC in the 21st century might have changed the way correspondents report about political sources. This book is novel in its approach to empirically map the dimensions of a transnational journalism culture, with DC providing the ideal case for such an analysis. The empirical study elaborates on the source-reporter relationship in a new transnational environment. Before explaining the details of the study, it is necessary to understand what is currently known about journalism culture and the importance of moving toward a more transnational, connected, and multicultural approach of studying the source-reporter relationship to theorize journalism culture.

State of the Art on Journalism Culture

Most studies on journalism culture have looked at journalists functioning in a particular social system. For example, scholars in various countries surveyed journalists' perception of their professional roles and work (e.g., Keel, 2011; Marr, Wyss, Blum, and Bonfadelli, 2001; Weaver, Beam, Brownlee, Voakes, and Wilhoit, 2007; Weaver and Wilhoit, 1986, 1996; Weischenberg, Malik, and Scholl, 2006), compared different journalism cultures (Hanitzsch, 2011; Quandt, Löffelholz, Weaver, Hanitzsch, and Altmeppen, 2006), and examined foreign correspondents working in a different social system than the ones in which their news organizations are based (Peterson, 1979; Willnat and Weaver, 2003). This direction of research is to be expected, considering that theories explaining levels of influence on news such as Gatekeeping Theory (e.g., Shoemaker and Vos, 2009) have rested on the assumption of five levels of influence, in which social systems (e.g., culture, nation-state, individual history of countries) represent the outermost level. Such theoretical and analytical models like Gatekeeping Theory have the power to direct and organize the research findings. For example, the nation-state is considered to shape the individual professional attitudes of journalists. Most studies on journalism culture argue that journalists from different countries are different because they work in different countries under different political and economic structures. However, the privatization of television and convergence toward the US model has led scholars to conclude that distinctions among social systems have disappeared while a global ideal is appearing (Benson and Hallin, 2007), which would question the application of theoretical models like Gatekeeping Theory by taking the nation-state as the basis of comparison. One of the contemporary paradigms in comparative media research results from such a paradoxical coexistence of the differences and the universal (i.e., the West and the Global) in media structures and media content across the globe (Wahl-Jorgensen and Hanitzsch, 2009): National borders may no longer draw distinctions among media cultures, but differences in media cultures might be based on cultural, linguistic, or ethnic criteria, which may cross over national borders. Waisbord (2004) argued that global and national media trends are not necessarily contradictory to each other but can also complement one another. Furthermore, global trends in national media contexts reflect internal struggles of a media industry in how "the globalization of the business model of television and the efforts of international and domestic companies deal with the resilience of national cultures" (Waisbord, 2004, p. 360). Hence, the next step in journalism research is to empirically investigate such global or transnational journalism cultures to understand how globalization affects journalism cultures. Now, to understand the phenomena, we have to first map out a way to approach the concept of transnational journalism culture and a definition of the meaning of *journalism culture* and *transnational journalism*. The coherent understanding of the concepts will set the road map for the empirical study and build new knowledge on journalists' relationship with sources in the 21st century.

Journalism Culture

Understanding journalism cultures is important because of its impact on news coverage (Graber, 2002). However, Hanitzsch's (2007a) conceptualization of journalism culture still rests on the idea that journalism culture corresponds to the country in which those journalists work. On the other hand, there is clearly a need for an elaborated theoretical foundation on which transnational journalism cultures can be analyzed and explained. For example, why do foreign correspondents have less access to important policy makers than US correspondents? How does less access affect the coverage of US politics?

Journalism culture is considered "a particular set of ideas and practices by which journalists legitimate their role in society and render their work meaningful" (Hanitzsch, 2007a, p. 369). In a transnational news environment, we might wonder what journalists' meaning of society entails: What specific context are journalists referring to as "society"? Are they referring to a society from their home country where journalists were born and raised or where they were socialized (e.g., their first job), or is a transnational context creating its own logic of such a multicultural society? Is a class of cosmopolitan journalists (i.e., Reese, 2001) emerging?

Hanitzsch's (2007a) theoretical piece published in *Communication Theory* has greatly contributed to contemporary understandings of how to operationalize journalism culture. He identified three basic levels that articulate journalism culture: the performative, the evaluative, and the cognitive (see table 1.1). The performative level (i.e., journalists' practice) is defined as how journalists select, report, and frame stories; journalism culture is materialized in the way journalists do their work. The evaluative and the cognitive levels structure the way journalists perform their job (e.g., whether or not they seek balance in reporting). At the evaluative level, journalism cultures manifest themselves by professional worldviews or role conceptions of journalists. An evaluative level may serve prescriptive functions, as it functions as a normative guideline. In fact, a large body of literature examines role

Table 1.1   The Three Levels of Transnational Journalism Culture

Cognitive Level	Performative Level	Evaluative Level
Perception and interpretation.	Methods of reporting.	Professional worldviews.
Attribution of news values to events and/or sources.	Interaction with politicians.	Professional Roles.
	News Coverage.	

Source: Adapted from Hanitzsch, 2007, p. 369.

conceptions or professional worldviews, mostly with an underlying normative assumption that evaluative elements as part of a journalism culture will eventually inform performative elements of a journalism culture (e.g., Graber, 2002; Hanitzsch, 2011; Shoemaker and Reese, 1996). The cognitive level bridges the evaluative and performative levels. At the cognitive level, journalism culture is shaped by a structure on which perception and attribution of news values to events is based. As such, the cognitive level is very much a component of the performative level, if performative elements are not solely to be analyzed on an output level but also with regard to how journalists perform their jobs, how they select sources, and how they gather news.

Schudson (2001) further distinguished between practices and norms that inform journalistic practices. In essence, journalism scholarship implicitly pays attention to the importance of the two components of a journalism culture: evaluative (norms) and performative (practice). However, journalism scholarship has mostly treated the two as independent fields of investigation. One strand of journalism research has focused on news values, news factors (i.e., indicators), source selection, and frames in news reports by content-analyzing performative elements of journalism (Iyengar, 1991; Strömbäck and Dimitrova, 2006; Tresch, 2009). Another strand of research has investigated journalists' role perception or journalism's institutional role (i.e., its evaluative component). Journalistic role conception has been defined as journalists' perception of journalism's social functions in society (Donsbach, 2008b; Weaver et al., 2007). Those perceived social functions are assumed to shape the stories that journalists ultimately report, but a normative link between role conception and role enactment should be met with skepticism (Tandoc, Hellmueller, and Vos, 2013). In fact, media organizations are influenced by the demands of external factors such as financial concerns and competition with other media (Shoemaker and Vos, 2009). To understand the multilevel concept of journalism culture, its practice and norms have to be considered. Hanitzsch's (2007a) framework for conceptualizing journalism culture around the world remains on the evaluative level. He and his colleagues surveyed journalists in over 80 countries and asked them about their professional roles (worldsofjournalism.org), but they have not linked those statements to actual practices. To shed light on the concept of journalistic culture, this book approaches it empirically from the source-reporter relationship and analyzes those different levels of journalism culture to conceptualize, operationalize, and empirically investigate Hanitzsch's (2007a) conceptualization of levels of journalism cultures—in a transnational context.

Transnational Journalism

Globalization has affected journalism at all levels. As Reese (2008) argued, globalization exists in many different forms and facets so that even a newswire in Africa using the Internet as a research tool can be considered an example of how globalization affects news gathering. Aligned to this trend, Wiley (2004) suggested that the nation-state should be considered one variable among many others to organize social space. That is not to say that the global has replaced the local, but that organizing principles of news gathering have changed because journalism news-gathering methods and practices have transcended national boundaries (Reese, 2008). For example, foreign correspondents in DC gather news for an audience near and far, but they also adapt to news-gathering principles in the capital, which might be different from the expectations of their news organization at home. DC may have different protocols and expectations of press conferences, a different way of interacting with sources, and a different intensity of competition such as journalists competing to ask a question at a White House press conference. In that sense, transnational journalism in this book refers to that news-gathering culture beyond national borders, when journalists are basing their news-gathering criteria not solely on nation-state practices but are being immersed in a transnational environment such as DC. Transnational is thus different from global, the word describes how journalism can be understood from transcending national boundaries, that is, the local aspect might still be very visible, but not as a sole criterion. On the other hand, when considering global aspects of journalism, we are more interested in finding unifying ideas or principles that unite journalism around the world. Transnational journalism culture may well express similar ideas as global journalism, but in transnational journalism, journalists may well remain resilient to contextual pressure and still embrace the kind of journalism they learned in their home country instead of adapting to global practices and ideals in a deterministic matter because the context has changed.

The 21st Century: The Importance of Relationships

The focus of this book lies on the relationship between reporters and political sources in DC. It is those interactions that demonstrate expressions of journalists' strong beliefs and ideals of working in a transnational news environment. Correspondents depend on their sources as resources of information. However, in past decades, the traditional role of journalists as gatekeepers who control the public's access to information has shifted to a nonlinear, interactive idea of journalism in a networked society, particularly in the Western world. This is partly due to globalization because technology enables a variety of people to take up reporting (Singer, 2010). Thus, journalists no longer necessarily hold a privileged gatekeeping position but are instead thrown into a network of relationships. In a networked society, interactions and relationships with other information providers become salient. Singer (2007) argued that with journalism becoming increasingly less dependent on organizational structures, the reporter becomes more independent from organizational constraints. The journalist's work then focuses on applying professional norms to relationships that he or she holds with sources and interactions within such a network. Hence, interpersonal factors become important when moving from a profession of gatekeeping to a profession that cultivates social relations. For example, journalists are more likely to grant favorable news coverage to credible sources, which can have serious implications for establishing media frames of their sources (Yoon, 2005). Studies show that journalists consider officials from their home countries to be more credible and newsworthy than officials from foreign countries (Seo and Lim, 2008; Yoon, 2005). Indeed, interpersonal communication theory has pointed to the relationship between perceived homophily (i.e., similarity that a receiver perceives to exist between him and an information source) and source credibility (e.g., Allen and Post, 2004; J. C. McCroskey, Richmond, and Daly, 1975; L. L. McCroskey, McCroskey, and Richmond, 2006). Because the news media influence the public's perception of politicians, it is crucial to look at journalists' social relations with sources to understand how journalists frame politicians. Gatekeeping Theory provides a holistic and exhaustive overview of the news-making process (e.g., Donsbach, 2008a; Shoemaker, 1991; Shoemaker and Vos, 2009). According to the most recent and comprehensive overview on gatekeeping research (Shoemaker and Vos, 2009), five levels of analysis can be predictive of news media content: the individual (e.g., norms, values, the individual disposition of journalists), the routines, the organization (e.g., media ownerships), the influence of social institutions (e.g., influences from government), and the social system (e.g., cultural influences).

One aim of this research is to understand individual-level influences—individual perceptions of an information source—to reconceptualize individual perceptions in relation to the other levels of gatekeeping in a transnational news environment. In other words, these levels define resources that journalists can draw from. For example, a news organization's economic resources (i.e., organizational-level influences) may define the news-gathering processes (i.e., routines-level influences), because a news organization's financial situation can influence the amount of time journalists have to contact sources and work on a story. Journalists' autonomy may certainly be determined by the medium, but their relations or interactions with sources may also be influenced by interpersonal variables apart from the media organization (e.g., Allen and Post, 2004; J. C. McCroskey et al., 1975; L. L. McCroskey et al., 2006). This book provides an empirical answer to those theoretically derived assumptions about the source-reporter relationship based on data collected from one of the most influential beats in Washington, DC: the political beat. Reflecting on 60 years of journalism theories, the book conceptualizes three major elements of the source-correspondent relationship within a transnational journalism culture that set the theoretical framework of transnational journalism culture. It also sheds new knowledge on two important developments based on the idea of an emerging global world: first, it maps out how globalization has affected the way journalists from around the globe gather news in Washington, DC, competing for source access, exclusive information, and competing for gaining trust of political (mostly US) sources. Second, it theorizes how evolving journalistic practices in a transnational environment affect our theoretical assumptions of journalism. Based on a one-year research study, it proposes three elements of transnational journalism culture, outlining the relationship between correspondent and their sources in a global environment, which explain the theoretical underpinning of a transnational journalism culture when taking the network level of analysis. Using the network level of analysis, we can conceptualize the three elements of a transnational journalism culture as indicated in table 1.1.

Cognitive Level: From a cognitive level, the study analyzes how perceptions of journalists influence news judgments of political sources and what role cultural closeness to a source plays in how sources are eventually framed in news. Cultural closeness is an important variable to consider, as it might provide an alternative to the nation-state unit. By looking at cultural closeness, we move from a dichotomous variable (foreign or not) to a continuous form of understanding cultural similarity and difference (paying attention to the fact that a foreign correspondent can feel culturally closer than another foreign correspondent). For sure, some foreign correspondents have lived in the United States for more than 20 years, whereas others have lived there for less than five years. Some are married to US citizens, whereas some have become US citizen themselves; also, some are more fluent in the English than others. All these factors lead to the conclusion that it is impossible to group these correspondents together in one group, as they are too diverse. Rather, the study aims to explain cultural similarity in its full spectrum. One European correspondent explained the differences among foreign correspondents as follows:

> What's always bothering me a little bit is how my colleagues are so critical of the United States. I feel that every foreign correspondent is a little biased against the US, because the US is a big and rich country. So each time they get a chance to say something mean against the US, they would never miss such a chance. I find that a little irritating, because it does not hurt them to say something nice about the US. My situation is of course very different, in a sense that I have been here for a long time. I care for this country. For us foreign reporters, it is very important to live in an American environment. I'm very Americanized. The feeling of the mainstream gives me an idea how Americans feel about the economy and the political life. (personal communication, January 2012, Washington, DC)

Foreign correspondents may resist change and remain ethnocentric in their perspectives, even after living in the United States for a couple of years. The second level of journalism culture explains how their attitudes may affect their interactions with sources. The performative level further elaborates on constraints—apart from journalists' attitudes and perception—which impact professional news coverage.

Performative Level: While transnational journalism spaces have existed since the evolving practice of foreign correspondence by the early 1800s, advances in communication technologies have affected foreign correspondents' interactions with sources and the stories they produce. The first part of this book conceptualizes source access in a transnational journalism environment, outlining what constraints journalists face and how it differs from a national journalism context. It contextualizes journalism practices by outlining under what conditions news is produced in DC and how journalists' interaction with sources influences their reporting.

Evaluative Level: The evaluative level refers to professional ideologies and role conceptions of journalists. This level outlines how national journalism cultures may merge under transnational structures (global) and what remains the same (i.e., which national differences may still coexist). Even though multiculturalism as a professional ideology has emerged on local, national, and global levels of reporting, it is most critical on global levels, where audiences still rely very heavily on media coverage because of lack of immediate contacts. Journalists face choices about how to cover cultural conflicts and how to arrive at ethical judgments when covering immigration issues in DC, for example. Such choices are difficult and involve "hard choices between upholding our own cultural values and considering the values of other cultures" (Ting-Toomey and Chung, 2005, p. 335). These choices implicitly guide decisions of whether or not journalists embrace metaethical decision-making processes. Metaethical decisions refer to cultivating choices that transcend any particular ideological position (i.e., epistemological reflexivity). This book maps out how multiculturalism is another important element shaping the source-correspondent relationship. Furthermore, the book poses some of those ethical dilemmas, which can stimulate critical thinking and testing of multiple outcomes and consequences.

The Correspondents Selected for the Study

The question of who are the news gatekeepers is an ongoing debate among scholars and practitioners. Shoemaker and Vos (2009) pointed out that information in blogs or on citizen journalism websites are highly redundant and could not have been experienced firsthand. Although new competitors have operated at lower journalistic standards, they have also forced mainstream journalists to renegotiate their positions in the field where resources are increasingly scarce and audience attention is dwindling.

The book bases its empirical investigation on US and foreign Washington correspondents who report for a national audience on a daily basis. From May 2011 through January 2012, the different elements of a transnational journalism culture were examined using a representative web survey and follow-up qualitative interviews. Mixing research methodologies is important because "the field advances more assuredly when opposing paradigms are combined in the same theoretical framework and data analysis" (Hage, 2004, p. xv). By conducting a web survey that analyzes how journalists' perceptions influence their reporting about politicians, journalism's performative element can be studied. With an in-depth analysis that followed the web survey, the evaluative element of journalism could be studied and combined as an explanatory element along with the performative part. All identification of research participators remains anonymous, consistent with research procedures.

Structure of the Book

The second chapter builds on an in-depth conceptualization of the levels of transnational journalism culture, outlining the major challenges and constitutive elements of a reporter-source relationship in a transnational news environment. The main objective of the third chapter is to examine the evolving importance of foreign journalists in DC to conceptualize a framework of multiculturalism as a professional ideology and to address it from journalists' experience of working with various international sources. In the final chapters, the book addresses what has changed in news gathering in a national context to prepare future journalists working under such constraints and opportunities. The conclusion provides a resource for scholars to think anew about transnational journalism. It synthesizes disaggregate parts of what we know about journalism culture and proposes a new framework of transnational journalism. The proposed model of transnational journalism culture explains the need to conceptualize the source-correspondent relationship based on those levels shaping the news environment in DC. Perception and interpretation (i.e., the cognitive level) explain how cultural similarity matters in how correspondents perceive politicians; professional roles and ideologies (i.e., the evaluative level) explain how correspondents aim to interact with politicians and which sources they value; and the performative level explains how the performance of correspondents is constrained as well as encouraged by specific news-gathering structures in the capital, such as access rules for US and foreign correspondents. Not least, the model outlines the linkage between levels. How do correspondents' perceptions matter for their interaction (i.e., combining the cognitive with the performative level)? How do different truth-telling ideologies manifest in correspondents' sourcing choices (i.e., explaining the performative level with the evaluative level)?

The empirical study of correspondents in Washington, DC explains how journalists from various countries navigate in a transnational environment and how well those global journalists meet and reshape the normative standards of the future. DC will remain an important headquarter for international and national reporting; as one US correspondent expressed his fascination for reporting from the capital, "And then coming to Washington was like coming to Broadway. That is how I felt about Washington; I always wanted to come. Always. And I never left again." (personal communication, January 2012).

2

Correspondents' Perceptions and Interactions with DC Sources

Even if you get to become friends with a politician, it's all about your responsibility of being able to make the difference between your personal relationship with him or her and your professional duties of honesty and independence.

—Foreign correspondent, personal communication,
Washington, DC, January 2012

This chapter explains how social relations between politicians and correspondents shape what is on the news and, more specifically, how the relationship between correspondents and their sources matters for how a politician is portrayed in the news. As an element of transnational journalism culture, the cognitive aspect and practice of news gathering evolves as a first component of understanding the source-reporter relationship in DC. At a cognitive level, journalistic cultures are expressed through the perception and interpretation of sources. In the DC case, the cognitive level examines how the cultural background of US and foreign correspondents influences their perceptions of politicians' credibility and newsworthiness. What are the patterns of how journalists perceive politicians? How do their cultural backgrounds influence the perception of politicians' credibility? This might be less a question of journalistic culture and more of culture per se. Donsbach (1987) recognized that subjective factors such as culture also matter for the news content that media professionals produce. Journalists' perceptions materialize in their work and in their methods of reporting through professional performance (Hanitzsch, 2007a). Here again, personal characteristics might influence their professional performance, such as the journalists' foreign status limiting their access to White House press conferences. However, subjective factors such as cultural background are becoming part of their journalism culture, shaping their daily job duties.

Based on correspondents' perceptions and interpretations, this chapter further investigates how those cognitive-level variables influence the interactions between correspondents and politicians in the 21st century. The cognitive level explores how journalists perceive politicians. How credible and culturally similar do DC correspondents perceive politicians to be? Is there a difference between foreign and US correspondents in how credible they perceive their sources? The performative level inquires how those perceptions manifest themselves in journalistic performance (i.e., how journalists report, gather news, and use sourcing): How do correspondents' perceptions of a source's credibility influence the tone of the story? How does cultural similarity influence how journalists interact with politicians (e.g., whether they have personal access to politicians)?

The Cognitive and Performative Levels of Journalism Culture

The study empirically tested how US and foreign correspondents interact with US politicians (broadly identified as those who carry a political function in DC, regardless of how they came to hold the current position) and how cultural differences affect US and foreign correspondents' perceptions of politicians' credibility in Washington, DC. Hence, this study seeks to understand whether a transnational news-gathering environment reduces cultural differences or whether it instead brings to light those differences even more because journalists can see what other correspondents are doing or how much access to political sources they enjoy. For example, if foreign correspondents have become very familiar with the US news environment, are they more likely to perceive politicians in DC as credible sources? Hence, the focus of this second chapter is on the cognitive and performative levels of a journalism culture in DC.

News is a highly collaborative process, and for many correspondents, their most important sources of information are their personal contacts. While those relationships can be shaped by correspondents' cultural backgrounds, other factors such as financial resources may play an important role in cultivating news sources. For example, news organizations that can afford to pay sources for exclusive information may choose that route, which hinders other journalists from getting in touch with the same sources. In fact, examples of paying sources for exclusive information or material include the case when ABC News paid $200,000 to Casey Anthony, the Florida woman accused of killing her 2-year-old daughter, for exclusive rights to videos and pictures that ran on its network. Another example is CNN, which paid $10,000 for the rights on an image taken by Jasper Schuringa, a Dutch citizen who overpowered an alleged Christmas Day bomber. Hence, another important empirical question is whether secondhand news sources (sources quoted in other media) influence correspondents' perception of those sources; if so, in which direction? Journalists' relationship with a source may shape the way they cover the news. If they conduct a personal interview, then the source's sound bite may be prioritized over a news report from another news organization. The empirical question remains: How does the source-correspondent relationship affect the coverage of political sources in DC, if at all?

This chapter first sets a theoretical background of what is known about sourcing in a transnational news environment and then provides a theoretical linkage between perception and news, specifically in how sourcing influences news reporting. This chapter is designed to theorize the individual level (i.e., the correspondent) in linkage with the social system (i.e., the cultural background) to understand gatekeeping in a transnational news environment. The individual level of measurement consists of surveys with journalists as well as qualitative interviews, and the individual and social-system levels of analysis explain the outcomes based on the social-system background of those journalists. For this purpose, the news environment in Washington, DC is analyzed to examine how personal characteristics and cultural variables of gatekeeping provide structure to the practices of DC correspondents as a whole. Most studies have examined a subgroup of correspondents, but this book is novel in examining both US and foreign correspondents. By looking at the overall DC corps, differences and similarities between nationalities can be empirically investigated.

Outline of the Chapter

Because journalists speak through their sources (Reese, 1990), most professional characteristics of correspondents become visible when journalists interact with sources. Thus, it makes the most sense to start an analysis of transnational journalism where we witness most of journalistic professionalism: the journalists' interactions with sources. It can be concluded that cultural differences reveal themselves in journalists' understanding of their professional relationship with sources. This chapter examines sourcing in a transnational news environment and the implication of the reporter-source relationship on news content.

The chapter opens with a description of the DC media corps in the 21st century, followed by a description of the DC corps investigated for this research: How were the data collected? Who are US and foreign correspondents? For which media do they work? Where do they come from? How long have they been in DC? All these questions will be addressed before presenting the results about how those journalists perceive politicians, how cultural similarity matters for their reporting, and how their interactions with politicians shape their attitudes toward those news sources.

The DC Media Corps in the 21st Century

The last comprehensive study on the DC press corps dates back to 2009. The Project for Excellence in Journalism investigated the press corps over a three-month period in 2009 and published a report titled "The New Washington Press Corps: As Mainstream Media Decline, Niche and Foreign Outlets Grow" (Pew, 2009). Although those findings might be already outdated, they provide a good overview of the DC press corps before the turn of the 21st century. The conclusions of the study included three major findings: one, a significant decrease in the reporting power of mainstream media, mainly because from the mid-1980s to 2008, the number of newspapers has fallen by more than half and newspaper reporters accredited to cover congress has declined 30 percent. The second finding is that "the decline in mainstream press has been nearly matched by a sharp growth among more narrowly focused special interest or niche media" (Pew, 2009, p. 3). More specialty newspapers, magazines, and newsletters are in the capital, and staff from these outlets accredited to Congress grew nearly 50 percent between 1997 and 2009. The third trend is "a marked jump in foreign media now represented in Washington" (Pew, 2009, p. 3). In 2008, there were nearly ten times the foreign media than in 1968 when the US State Department first opened a Foreign Press Center. However, as the Pew research shows, foreign journalists still lack access to key federal government decision makers and thus publish fewer stories of significance, compared to US correspondents. The growth is more a broadening than a deepening of their news, but the presence of foreign media has strong implications for what the world knows about the United States. The Pew study (2009) pointed out that the executive branch of the federal government has also contributed to the shift of media serving more specialized and elite interests as the federal government is becoming more circumspect, secretive, and combative when dealing with media. The declining numbers of regional newspaper bureaus also mean that entire state congressional delegations might be underreported in news because fewer regional newspapers are present in the capital. The rise of niche media has affected the flow of talented reporters in DC that for decades ran from these smaller interest papers to mainstream newsrooms. The flow is in the opposite direction today, with reporters moving from mainstream newsroom to niche publications or online newsletters.

Much of the growth in foreign correspondents is from China, the Middle East, and Africa, where American policies have become more important over the past several years (Pew, 2009). Both invasions, the one in Afghanistan and that in Iraq, have increased interest from media outlets, especially from the Middle East. The BBC, with about 50 staff members, still maintains one of the largest news bureaus in DC and produces programs for a US audience such as World News America. What people are learning about the United States and its policies is still significantly decided by those foreign correspondents who gather news "on the ground." But their power is limited: the impact of the foreign media on DC is considered marginal despite its growth, and foreign journalists struggle for access to key sources; BBC for example, tried for months without success to obtain interviews with presidential candidates in 2008 (Pew, 2009). Broader rather than deeper coverage brings to light new empirical questions about source-reporter relationships in DC and reveals some paradoxes about foreign reporting in the 21st century. Such findings might be surprising because it would be reasonable to assume that new technologies and recent economic crises might have altered source-reporter relationships, particularly in industrialized societies. However, with the widening availability of information via the Internet and social media such as Twitter and Facebook, access might not be the key to success anymore. In a digitized media environment such as the United States, a drastic decrease in communication costs (e.g., Lewis, 2010) has threatened the exclusive access to political sources crucial to journalism's professional prestige and thus may have altered journalists' relationships with sources. Interactions between politicians and journalists have become more institutionalized as part of the journalism profession, and journalists now live in a networked society where source access no longer seems as prestigious as before. Does this situation point to greater access for foreign correspondents to politicians in Washington, DC? That would be contradictory to other studies' findings citing that most foreign correspondents express frustration regarding lack of access to sources. As noted by Willnat and Weaver (2003), "A large majority (79%) said that they have had problems obtaining information from U.S. sources because they are foreign correspondents and not American journalists" (p. 414). On the other hand, the relationship between access to sources, the quality of the relationship, and the exclusive availability of sources for journalists should be met with new skepticism. It might well be that source access does not guarantee exclusive information to journalists in every instance or that information is no longer exclusively shared with one news organization.

Paradoxically though, the economic instability of the news business might contribute to reporters' dependence on exclusive credible sources to do their jobs because news scoops still remain the number-one indicator of success in journalism. Thus, sources remain an important resource to enhance journalism's economic capital. In addition, a normative shift toward transparency (Hellmueller, Vos, and Poepsel, 2013) in the journalism field enhances the importance of information from credible sources, because it has never been easier to detect false information than in an open-access society such as the United States.

The Sampling Procedure

There is no single definitive, comprehensive database that lists every news organization based in Washington, DC. Nevertheless, there are sources such as directories that list a significant percentage of reporters and news organizations. After consulting with a variety of former and current journalists working in Washington, DC, the decision was made to work with *Hudson's Washington News Media Contacts Directory 2010* (Mars, 2009). The directory has been published annually since 1968 and lists all news organizations in Washington, DC by category of the medium. Because a major concern of this study was to look at source-reporter interactions, the physical presence in DC applied to all correspondents chosen for this study.

News organizations represented in Washington, DC, vary in different categories: type of medium, national or regional/local or niche audience, quality or tabloid papers, and electronic media according to ownership (e.g., public, state owned, and privately owned). To gather data from correspondents working for a variety of news organizations, the use of a stratified sampling method helped to avoid oversampling one group of correspondents working for the same news organization. Newsrooms were selected along two first-level parameters.

First, news organizations that produce political news for national audiences were included. Second, a distinction was drawn between countries of origin. It was assumed that the number of US Washington journalists working for the big outlets was slightly lesser than 2,000. The number of foreign Washington correspondents was about 1,500. Thus, the total percentage of DC correspondents equaled 42.86 percent for foreign correspondents and 57.14 percent for US correspondents. The percentage of the population of each group provided the sampling size of each group. From each news organization, people listed in the directory as political correspondents were selected first. If that label did not apply to anyone working for a particular news organization, then reporters or news reporters were chosen. All names of correspondents listed in the 2010 edition of *Hudson's Washington News Media Contacts Directory* (Mars, 2009) were compiled into an Excel file before the exact sample size was defined. In this study, the unit of analysis was the correspondent or reporter. Table 2.1 shows how the sample of correspondents was stratified based on their news organizations.

The population of correspondents ($N = 620$) coded from the directory consisted of 373 US Washington correspondents and 247 foreign Washington correspondents. To account for errors in the directory, editors or bureau chiefs were also coded, but only if there were no correspondents or political reporters listed for that news organization. Using this compiled list, notification letters were dispatched to those people, asking them to report whether there was someone else working at their news organization who better fit the criteria of "mainly dealing with political reporting on a day-to-day basis." To address sourcing in a transnational news environment, a web survey was conducted to first describe and then predict sourcing in a transnational news environment.

Table 2.1   Coding Sheet for the Stratified Sampling Method

Country of Origin	News Organization	Job Title
This category did not ask for the place of birth but for the location of the news organization. Correspondents from the United States were coded as 1, and foreign correspondents were coded as string variables with their original countries (e.g., F_Italy). Doing this allowed the grouping of countries in different categories (level of press freedom, developed vs. developing, and regions).	The full name of the news organization was coded. Another variable coded the medium. The revision of categories resulted in the organization of new groups. However, the results of the survey were anticipated to reveal whether or not additional categories are needed and how much they overlap. 1 = Newspaper 2 = Magazine 3 = TV 4 = Radio 5 = Web-Based Media 6 = Wire Service	In this category, all correspondents who interact with politicians were coded. The initial plan was to exclude editors and code the correspondents. If that job title did not apply, the political reporter was coded. If that still did not apply, the job that seemed to offer the highest levels of interactions with politicians was coded. To control for the heterogeneity of job titles, the original job title was also coded as a string variable. The exact job titles were taken from the *Hudson Washington News Media Contacts Directory* (Mars, 2009).

Table 2.2   Steps of Implementation

Advance Notification	Advance Notification 2	Actual Survey	Second mailing	Third mailing	Reminder calls
Day 0	Day 7	Day 8	Day 13	Day 19	Day 25

The advanced e-mail notifications helped to achieve an accurate estimate of valid e-mail addresses from US and foreign correspondents in Washington, DC. After eliminating the invalid e-mail addresses, a list of 460 contacts provided the sample frame for this study. However, further problems remained: some of the addresses were general ones targeted toward a newsroom, some of the names were misspelled, journalists no longer worked at the same jobs, or the media organization had closed down the DC office (for the timeline, see table 2.2).

After completion of the data-gathering process, 158 valid responses were collected. One major concern was to achieve an equivalent number of responses from the two groups (i.e., foreign and US correspondents)

so that the validity of the findings would be increased. The response rate of 33.70 percent can be considered acceptable because the main concern of this research was to prevent response bias by accounting for an equal number of US and foreign correspondents.

Journalists Included in this Study

In terms of demographics, this study included 43.9 percent US correspondents and 55.7 percent foreign correspondents.[1] From both groups, 62.6 percent were males. From the total sample, 58 percent reported that they had been working in the DC area for more than nine years (see table 2.3). One may conclude that these journalists were experienced correspondents because they were covering one of the most important political beats in the world. This resonates with Willnat and Weaver's (2003) observation that "most of the foreign correspondents based in Washington or New York represent the best and brightest of their profession in their native countries" (p. 404).

Correspondents were asked to indicate all media organizations for which they provided news content. The majority of the participants, 52.9 percent, worked for a newspaper. In general, most of the surveyed correspondents worked for one medium (71.1%). However, they may be working for several news organizations at the same time (e.g., providing content for two newspapers, which is the same medium but two different news organizations). The idea of news becoming more a story told by a journalist instead of being a product of one media organization is an emerging trend: more than 23 percent of all the correspondents reported that their work went to more than one medium. This trend of reporting a story across different media reflects the growing importance of multimedia journalism in journalism curricula across education institutions.

Table 2.3   Correspondents' Years of Professional Experiences in DC (N = 155)

Years in DC	N	Percentage
1 year or less	7	4.5
More than 1 year, but less than 3 years	25	16.1
3 years or more, but less than 5 years	20	12.9
5 years or more, but less than 9 years	19	12.3
9 years or more	84	54.2

Transnational Audiences: Reporting Globally

An important dynamic based on a multimedia ideal of journalism is the emergence of a transnational audience. Whereas foreign correspondents in the past have reported for an audience in their respective countries of origin, this does not necessarily hold true anymore. Some foreign correspondents working in the United States report for a news organization based in their home country (e.g., Italy), but the reach of their work is not limited because their stories are also available to audiences outside of their countries via news blogs or on their media organization's website. For example, reporters of an Italian wire service ANSA (Agenzia Nazionale Stampa Associata) working in Washington, DC, not only report to audiences based in Italy but also provide a translated version of their articles in English on their news organization's website. Furthermore, ANSA reporters provide multimedia elements to their news stories (i.e., videos when accessible) and, in the 2012 US election year, they kept a news blog about the presidential election in the United States. Thus, there is a tendency for journalists to work in more than one medium at a time (see table 2.4).

Lack of Access for Foreign Reporters

The major complaint voiced by foreign correspondents covering the United States is a lack of access to US government sources (Willnat and Weaver, 2003). Indeed, the results of this study show that US and foreign correspondents differ in their news-gathering behavior. News-gathering behaviors provide a detailed picture of what kind of access distinguishes work between US and foreign correspondents. Foreign

Table 2.4   Media Worked by US and Foreign Correspondents (N = 214)

Medium	N	Percentage
Newspaper	82	52.9
TV	38	24.5
Newswire	29	18.7
Web	26	16.8
Magazine	20	12.9
Radio	19	12.3

Note: Correspondents could select multiple answers (i.e., "all that apply").

and US correspondents differ in their frequency of gathering information over the telephone and in their frequency of collecting information from other media. In fact, US correspondents (63.1%) are more likely to conduct an interview on the phone than foreign correspondents (37.3%): $\chi^2(1, N = 148) = 9.658, p =. 002$. Earlier studies have found that the most difficult challenge for foreign correspondents in DC is to get source access over the phone (Willnat and Weaver, 2003). Members of the Congress or US officials are "often unwilling to take the time to talk to foreign correspondents," and there is a general feeling among foreign correspondents that "U.S. officials generally don't care about the foreign press" (p. 414). In addition, foreign correspondents (44.6%) and US correspondents (24.6%) differ in collecting information from other media: $\chi^2(1, N = 148) = 6.320, p = .01$. Foreign correspondents rely more on other media's stories than US correspondents do. Based on this comparison between US and foreign correspondents working in the same environment, the results suggest that lack of access becomes evident in their news-gathering methods. Foreign correspondents depend more on other media's reporting than US correspondents working in DC. Furthermore, US correspondents conduct significantly more phone interviews than foreign correspondents. Overall, by looking at the DC media corps as a whole, in-person interviews and phone interviews are the most frequent news-gathering methods, followed by the consultation of official documents and the gathering of information from other media (see table 2.5). The results support findings about the amount of high autonomy embodied by journalists in Washington, DC.

Table 2.5   US and Foreign Correspondents' News-Gathering Methods in DC

News-Gathering Method	N	Percentage
Phone interview	74	57.4
In-person interview	73	56.6
Consulting official documents	62	48.1
Information gathered from other media	53	41.1
Attending a press conference	50	38.8
E-mail interview	44	34.1
Gathered from a politician's blog or website	41	31.8
Quoting a press release	32	24.8
Quoting official websites	31	24.0
Information gathered from social media (e.g., Facebook, Twitter, etc.)	13	10.1

Note: The total number of responses was 473. The survey respondents could select multiple answers (i.e., "all that apply").

In fact, journalists in DC have reported a higher amount of job satisfaction and autonomy (62%) compared to US journalists as a whole across media (51%; Willnat and Weaver, 2003, p. 413).

The discussion of descriptive results helps illuminate working conditions of US and foreign correspondents in DC. However, descriptive results describe a situation without offering any explanation on how this may affect the work of correspondents in the political headquarters. For example, how does lack of access to US officials affect foreign correspondents' coverage of them? Are foreign correspondents more critical when they report on such sources because of perceived prejudice and discrimination (i.e., Willnat and Weaver, 2003) that may result from a lack of access—particularly if access is granted to their US counterparts?

Perceptions of Correspondents

The first dimension of sourcing in a transnational news environment dealt with how US and foreign correspondents assess political sources' credibility and homophily in Washington, DC (i.e., the cognitive level of transnational journalism culture). Theories are outlined as bases for their empirical findings. The results are presented to provide novel theoretical underpinning of source-reporter relationships in the 21st century.

Sourcing in a Transnational News Environment

People evaluate others from their own cultural vantage point. Gudykunst and Kim (2003) pointed out that one's cultural orientation acts as a filter for processing incoming and outgoing verbal and nonverbal messages. Neuliep, Hintz, and McCroskey (2005) took a same position: "To the extent that humans are ethnocentric, we tend to view other cultures (and microcultures) from our own cultural vantage point" (p. 44). Not only do people's cultural orientations influence their view of other cultures, but they also guide their interaction patterns. Given that more than three million minority-owned US businesses employ nearly five million workers (Neuliep, 2003), communicating with people from different cultures in an organizational context represents a daily challenge, where culture acts as a perceptual filter that affects the interpretation of verbal and nonverbal messages. Most important, in a journalism context, perceptions of sources are shaped through cultural filters, because no message is interpreted apart from its source (J. C. McCroskey and Richmond, 1996). Intercultural communication research has shown that the more the source and the receiver have similar backgrounds (i.e., homophilous), the more likely it is for communication attempts to increase and for communication to be effective based on perceived source credibility (J. C. McCroskey et al., 1975). Research in journalism studies has pointed in a similar direction, arguing that journalists' perception of source credibility is a strong predictor of source use (Schotz, 2008; Seo and Lim, 2008; Yoon, 2005). If multiculturalism represents an important dimension of journalists' professional ideology in the 21st century and source credibility remains an important news factor, the questions to be asked are as follows: How do journalists from different countries assess the credibility of politicians in Washington, DC, and how might that affect their reporting? Do intercultural dimensions such as perceived homophily and source credibility help explain journalists' perceptions of politicians and their news-gathering choices in Washington, DC?

When research focuses on sourcing and its implication for multiculturalism as a professional practice, there is a possibility that other challenges of journalism get ignored. Such challenges could include audiences' inclusion in the multicultural gatekeeping process to enhance their knowledge of diversity, technological changes that lead to a shifting of journalistic norms in an international environment (e.g., a normative shift from objectivity toward transparency), and the effects of changes toward a business media model (i.e., corporate media) on globalized newsroom policies and corporatization tendencies.

Nevertheless, sourcing is a very important and valid area to investigate because "the discourse of professional distance clearly stands in stark contrast to the rhetoric of inclusivity" (Deuze, 2005, p. 456). Thus, by opening the journalism field to sources from other cultures, a long-believed normative ideal of objectivity is contested because the autonomy of the field depends on a collaboration of sources to enhance journalists' understanding of multiculturalism, and their knowledge may eventually shape their representations of sources. Or to put it another way, because journalists need to engage with diverse sources, they may reduce the gap of their professional distance to enhance their knowledge about a particular culture. Therefore, multiculturalism calls for a normative adaption to the rhetoric of inclusivity. However, to understand how multiculturalism may become a professional practice, an empirical study on journalism culture—and more specifically, on how journalists select sources—in a multicultural environment provides the fuel to move beyond a normative discussion. Without doubt, such an analysis increases scholarly knowledge on what constitutes the basis for understanding journalism in a transnational news environment: the way journalists judge, select, and frame political sources from a variety of cultural backgrounds (i.e., the performative element of journalism culture). Thus, the concept of credibility is explained to set the framework for the empirical results that follow.

Credibility Research

Credibility is often used interchangeably with other constructs, particularly with the construct of trust. Some researchers use these two terms almost interchangeably. Kohring and Matthes (2007) advocated for trust over credibility to embed the construct in "theoretical concepts of society that transcend the simple identification of an information society" (p. 238). Following their argument, theories of trust refer to recipients' assessment on how societal functions of selecting and conveying information about interdependencies of modern societies are performed by the news media. Whereas trust research depends heavily on media's function in society (on a rather mezzo or macro level), credibility research relies more on interpersonal factors (i.e., source credibility on a micro level), on characteristics of the message source, or on characteristics of the medium through which the message is delivered. Hence, the distinction is drawn between sociology-based trust research that takes into consideration societal functions of media as a basis for a trust assessment and credibility research as a dimension for evaluating message sources (J. C. McCroskey and Young, 1979). Without doubt, the two constructs of credibility and trust enjoy high scholarly attention—credibility more so in the United States. It does not seem surprising, then, that the *American Behavioral Scientist* published an issue on credibility research in 2010 (Golan, 2010), and the *European Journal of Communication* put together a special issue on trust in 2012 (Golding, Sousa, and van Zoonen, 2012). This research argues that credibility and trust bear conceptual overlaps and are indeed interrelated, but for the sake of the conceptual clarity and reliability of our measures, this study analytically distinguishes between the two and hence focuses solely on credibility. Credibility research can be grouped into three different approaches: source credibility, media credibility, and message credibility (Metzger, Flanagin, Eyal, Lemus, and McCann, 2003). The locus of this investigation lies in the interpersonal communication process between journalists and political sources. Therefore, the source credibility concept is the focus of this review.

Source Credibility

The path-breaking study by Hovland and Weiss (1951) set the framework for credibility research, particularly for source credibility studies. The Yale Studies Program on Attitude Change was based on the former psychological studies of "prestige" (e.g., Arnett, Davidson, and Lewis, 1931), in which it was concluded that "the extent of agreement is usually higher when the statements are attributed to 'high prestige sources'" (Hovland and Weiss, 1951, p. 635). Hovland and Weiss adapted this basic idea and argued that the source (by *source*, they meant single persons, groups, organizations, or media) is a multidimensional predictor factor of communication effectiveness besides the content and the medium of a message. They observed that "opinions were changed immediately after the communication in the direction advocated by the communicator to a significantly greater degree when the material was presented by a trustworthy source than when presented by an untrustworthy source" (Hovland and Weiss, 1951, p. 650). The immediate reaction to the "fairness" of the presentation and the "justifiability" of the conclusion is significantly affected by the evaluation of sources' trustworthiness. Credibility came to be considered a universal characteristic of a general communication source, based on the two dimensions of credibility—*expertness* ("how well-informed and intelligent") and *trustworthiness* (Hovland, Janis, and Kelley, 1959).

Their conceptualization seems too simplistic in contemporary views because several variables of the message recipient were not taken into account. Cronkhite and Liska (1976) noted that the credibility of sources depends on the story topic and the specific function they perform in certain situations. Moreover, King (1976) captured a perspective that posits the varying relevance of source attributes as a function of the receiver's decision needs and message topics. Looking at source credibility, one does not only have to emphasize the perceived attributes but also the communication needs of the receiver or the potential function served by sources.

Since the 1970s, there has been an increasing precision in measurement from the seminal Yale studies to the factor analytical approach. A shift occurred from one-dimensional to multidimensional measures and from applying items of source credibility to applying specific items of media credibility (Kohring and Matthes, 2007).

On the other hand, J. C. McCroskey and Teven (1999) examined a body of literature on source credibility and argued that one dimension—goodwill—of the construct has been "lost." They argued that Aristotle's conceptualization of ethos/source credibility was based on three dimensions: competence, trustworthiness, and goodwill. They referred to Aristotle's conceptualization because it serves as a milestone in rhetorical communication theory. In fact, J. C. McCroskey and Teven's (1999) exhaustive empirical investigation with a variation of sources—from Madonna (celebrity), Gingrich (political figure), to the partner dated most recently (interpersonal source)—revealed that the amount of variance attributed to the goodwill and trustworthiness factors were more predictive than competence in how people came to believe a source. Hence, J. C. McCroskey and Teven (1999) argued that goodwill (i.e., perceived caring) is indeed a meaningful predictor of believability and likeableness and should take its place in the conceptual and operational future of communication research dealing with ethos and source credibility as a multidimensional construct.

Teven (2008) analyzed the perceived credibility of leading candidates for the US presidency in 2008. He was interested in finding out what contributes the most to the candidates' believability. The results showed that the perception of the candidate's goodwill is the most important characteristics for the public to believe politicians.

Goodwill is indeed a very important quality of any political source. A politician who relates well with voters is more likely to be perceived as a credible source (Teven, 2008). Existent research within a wide variety of contexts indicates that each dimension (competence, trustworthiness, and goodwill) contributes to important communication outcomes and effects (J. C. McCroskey and Teven, 1999; Teven, 2008). On the other hand, in a journalism context, the same question must be asked: Does the perception of source credibility contribute to important journalistic communication outcomes (e.g., media frames of politicians)? If journalists perceive politicians to care about their constituents, do they cover such sources more positively?

Ethos and Source Credibility

Qualities of character are crucially important to how politicians position themselves relative to others in communication. The rhetorical status therefore explains the continuing relevance of ethos. In Aristotle's art of persuasion, the term *ethos* (i.e., character in the Greek language) designates the image that the speaker presents of himself to exert an influence on his audience. At the core of Aristotle's rhetorical theory is his analysis of three modes of persuasion. These are commonly called *logos*, referring to discourse and reason; *pathos*, meaning the emotion aroused in the audience; and *ethos* (Yoos, 1979). Rhetorical theory applies the principle of ethos in two different forms. The first form is called "subjective ethos," meaning that the speaker exhibits qualities of a personal nature, intrinsic goodness and honesty, and an interest in the well-being of the audience that induces listeners to approve the arguments given in a speech (Sattler, 1947). He is explicit in giving the threefold bases of ethos. These are intellectual virtue, moral virtue, and goodwill (qualities that are in agreement with the customs and traditions of a social group; Sattler, 1947). Even though goodwill is closely allied with moral virtues, a second aspect of goodwill is related to characteristics that are basically nonmoral qualities: a speaker who resembles the audience, one who is clean and neat in dress, one who praises good qualities, one able and inclined to benefit the audience in a pecuniary way, or one who takes the audience seriously (Sattler, 1947). Hence, this also hints to the conceptual closeness of credibility and homophily (i.e., similarity).

Aristotle asserted that the speaker who possesses the three personal qualities of logos, pathos, and ethos will be worthy of belief (Sattler, 1947). To persuade an audience, intelligence, character, and goodwill are manifested by the choices the speaker makes. In looking at intelligence, character, and goodwill, it seems clear that the two constructs, source credibility and ethos, overlap. The two constructs differ in how they define ethos or source credibility and where they locate it, however. Hovland and Weiss's (1951) paradigm shifted the location of ethos from the source to the receiver. Ethos or source credibility was defined as receivers' image of a source. Aristotle, on the other hand, defined ethos as referring primarily to real or pretended qualities in the speaker, which must be seen from the speaker's view as well as from that of the audience (Sattler, 1947).

In other words, the persuasiveness of ethos depends on audience perceptions, but ethos itself belongs essentially to the speaker. Aristotle's main concern was to instruct speakers how to persuade an audience. He was referring to the human virtues, the qualities of mind or soul that depend on volition, moral esteem, and the "excellence" of a human being (Logue and Miller, 1995). On the other hand, source credibility focused on audience's responses and its acceptance to such an invention or speech—an ethos perceived in the eyes of others, in which the original meaning referred to ethos as belonging essentially to the speaker.

Nevertheless, the two constructs are interdependent because ethos is of importance to create a potential persuasive speech. Whether the speech is perceived as persuasive and effective, however, will only be decided on the receptor side—the source credibility end.

Perceived Homophily

Another important interpersonal factor is homophily, which is the degree of perceived similarity between the source and the receiver (J. C. McCroskey et al., 1975).

Looking at perceived homophily is important because perceived source credibility is not the only variable to influence communication outcomes: "In recent years, it has become generally accepted that cultural diversity in communicators' backgrounds makes a difference in communication behaviour" (Gudykunst, 1985a, p. 270). One construct that shifts cultural similarity from an either intra- or intercultural communication explanation to a more general explanatory construct is *perceived homophily* as it is applicable in either situation, in an intracultural or intercultural context (Gudykunst, 1985a). Kuhn (1970) pointed out that the more general a theory is, the longer it will last and the longer it will be accepted. The same may apply for perceived homophily as a theory-building construct of news gathering in a transnational news environment.

While studying the credibility of politicians, Teven (2008) suggested that perceived homophily with individual candidates may affect judgments of credibility. Communication effectiveness has been found to be influenced by how much the source and the receiver perceive themselves to be similar (L. L. McCroskey et al., 2006). Byrne (1971) argued that people evaluate positively those whom they perceive to hold similar attitudes and beliefs and negatively those whom they perceive to hold dissimilar attitudes and beliefs. There also appears to be a strong tendency to select receivers such as oneself in future interactions because the greater the dissimilarity between the cultures, the greater the likelihood that they will perceive each other as threatening (Prosser, 1978). Furthermore, a study by Wright (2000) pointed out that perceptions of similarity are related to judgments of credibility. Thus, one construct that is closely related to source credibility is *homophily*, which has been defined as the amount of perceived closeness or similarity that a receiver perceives as existing between oneself and an information source (L. L. McCroskey et al., 2006). The dimensions of attitude (i.e., perceived attitude similarity such as same values) and background homophily (i.e., perceived similarity in terms of economic situation, social class, similar childhood) have proven to be constant variables in subsequent research (J. C. McCroskey et al., 1975). Nevertheless, L. L. McCroskey et al. (2006) developed second-generation measures that are more reliable. Allen and Post (2004) pointed out that although there is considerable support for the persuasive impact of perceived similarity, only a few studies have explored this phenomenon in a political context. They conducted a study of voter preferences using source credibility, homophily, and attraction. Not all dimensions of source valence were highly correlated with candidate preferences. However, competence and attitude homophily were found to be significant predictors of voting behavior.

Measuring Credibility and Homophily

Although credibility seems to be one of the major variables in the process of communication, credibility studies have also received scholarly attention because of their lack of operational precision, the use of different items to measure the same construct, and insufficient reporting of reliability. Metzger et al. (2003) argued that

Table 2.6 Theoretical and Operational Definitions of Source Credibility

	Variable	Theoretical Definition	Operational Definition
Construct	Source Credibility	Attitude toward a source of communication held at a given time by a receiver.	Multidimensional construct, three dimensions.
Dimension	Competence	Perceived ability of the source to make valid assertions.	Six semantic differential items: intelligent, trained, expert, informed, competent, bright.
Dimension	Trustworthiness	Perceived willingness of the source to make valid assertions.	Six semantic differential items: honest, trustworthy, honorable, moral, ethical, genuine.
Dimension	Goodwill	The degree to which an audience perceives the source caring for them and having their best interest at heart.	Six semantic differential items: others' interests at heart, not self-centered, sensitive, understanding, concerned with the public, cares about others.

"disagreements about the relative importance of the dimensions of credibility led to the construction of various scales to measure this concept, each reflecting the priority of dimensions identified by particular researchers" (p. 298).

Disagreements derive from missing definitions of the credibility construct in empirical research: "The definition problem illustrated by the credibility research is a serious one, because many later decisions in factor analytic research must be based on the definition of the construct being studied" (J. C. McCroskey and Young, 1979, p. 376).

The three measures—competence, trustworthiness, and goodwill—represent unique dimensions but are correlated. Table 2.6 demonstrates source credibility factors that have been found to be reliable and valid in previous studies (Hickson, Hill, and Powell, 1979; Hovland and Weiss, 1951; J. C. McCroskey and Teven, 1999).

Perceived Homophily

Most effective communication occurs between people who have similar interests and a similar background. From a communication theory perspective, it has therefore been argued that effective communication, which results in fewer misunderstandings, is likely to occur between homophilous communicators. There also appears to be a strong tendency to select receivers like oneself in future interactions (Prosser, 1978). Homophily has also been studied in mediated communication contexts where Wright (2000) found that perceptions of source credibility and homophily were related to online network size and network satisfaction. L. L. McCroskey et al. (2006) produced second-generation measures with substantially improved internal reliability (see table 2.7).

Perceptions of Politicians' Source Credibility: Foreign vs. US correspondents

Foreign Washington correspondents seem to rate US politicians as slightly less credible than their US counterparts do, particularly on the trustworthiness and goodwill dimensions, but no significant differences were revealed between the two groups in how they assess the credibility of politicians in Washington, DC. At the beginning of this study, it was assumed that journalists in Washington, DC, most often communicate with sources from a US background (i.e., US citizens).

Table 2.7 Theoretical and Operational Definition of the Homophily Construct

	Variable	Theoretical Definition	Operational Definition
Construct	Homophily	Similarity that a receiver perceives as existing between himself and an information source.	Multidimensional construct (two dimensions).
Dimension	Attitude	Perceived attitude similarity such as same values.	14 items, Likert-type scale: thinks like me, behaves like me, shares my values, treats people like I do, has similar ideas, expresses similar attitudes, has a lot in common with me.
Dimension	Background	Perceived similarity in terms of personal history and social, economic, and cultural class.	10 items, Likert-type scale: social class, same status, economic situation, background, childhood, comes from a similar geographic region.

Although this held true for more than 90 percent of the correspondents, some sources working for the State Department, for example, were from foreign countries. The questionnaire of this current study asked correspondents to rate US news sources. However, a few correspondents did not refer to politicians with a US background when they answered the questionnaire about their most recent interaction with politicians in Washington, DC (i.e., US citizens or those with a long residency in the United States). The questionnaire began with an open-ended question that asked correspondents to describe their source interactions. The question was included to assess the nationality of the politicians. Hence, the results can only be generalized to DC politicians, most of whom were US citizens. The fact that the interaction took place between journalists of various cultural backgrounds who communicated with sources from a variety of cultures underlined the importance of studying interactions in a transnational context. It is possible to witness an increase in such multicultural interactions in which communication effectiveness may no longer only be explained by a country of origin variable (also see L. L. McCroskey, 2002, 2003). For that reason, the nature of political sources in Washington, DC, is discussed in more depth in the third chapter, presenting the findings based on conceptualizing a global journalism culture.

Source Credibility and Perceived Homophily

Based on the literature, it was assumed that perceived homophily with a political source will produce more positive perceptions of source credibility. The results show that journalists who perceived politicians to share the same values and attitudes as themselves perceived those sources as more competent, trustworthy, and caring than sources that did not share the same attitudes (see table 2.8).

Second, the results also provide an argument for the perception of credibility and its importance of shaping the tone or valence of the source in the news story. The strongest relationship was found for US Washington correspondents: tests of the relationships between valence of reporting revealed positive and strong associations in goodwill, $r(105) = .57, p < .001$; competence, $r(105) = .26, p < .001$; and trustworthiness, $r(105) = .65, p < .001$ for US Washington correspondents.

Table 2.8   Correlations Among Credibility and Homophily Scores

	CT	TW	GW	AH	BH
Source Credibility					
Competence (CT)	—	.57**	.50**	.42**	.13
Trustworthiness (TW)	.57**	—	.69**	.50**	.35**
Goodwill (GW)	.50**	.69**	—	.44**	.31**
Homophily					
Attitude Homophily (AH)	.42**	.50**	.44**	—	.34**
Background Homophily (BH)	.13	.35**	.31**	.34**	—

*Significant at the .05 level.
**Significant at the .001 level.

Table 2.9   Correlations Among Credibility and Valence of Reporting

	Goodwill	Competence	Trustworthiness
Valence of Reporting for the Total Sample	.35**	.26*	.28**
US Correspondents			
Valence of Reporting	.57**	.26*	.65**
Foreign Correspondents			
Valence of Reporting	.10	.28*	.13
Attitude Homophily	.44**	.42**	.50**
Background Homophily	.31**	.12	.35**

*Significant at the .05 level.
**Significant at the .001 level.

The study found support for a positive relationship between journalists' perceptions of a politician's credibility and favorable portrayal of the same political source in news content. In other words, if journalists perceive politicians to be competent, trustworthy, or caring about the public, the source's news coverage will be more favorable of the political source (see table 2.9).

Hence, we can identify one sourcing tendency based on those findings in a transnational news environment in Washington, DC:

Sourcing Dimension: Attitude Similarity Positively Affects the Perception of Source Credibility

The more US and foreign correspondents perceive themselves to be similar to a political source they are covering, the more they will perceive that source to be competent, trustworthy and caring about the audience. Hence, the more in common correspondents and sources have in terms of attitudes and values, the higher the source's credibility.

The Implication for the Performative Dimension

Gatekeeping Theory (Shoemaker and Vos, 2009) examines other levels of influence over news than cognitive or individual-level characteristics of journalists. Journalists' characteristics are embedded in an organization, and their behavior might be limited by routine or organizational structures. That is to say, other forces beside journalists' perceptions might be at work when journalists interact with sources. It is important to understand that news coverage is in most cases not solely based on one journalist's judgment. Editors in the newsroom, advertisers, and PR professionals, for example, might attempt to influence the tone of a story. Therefore, other factors have to be considered as well, which remain outside journalists' control. To account for forces that determine whether journalists' cognitive dimensions (i.e., their perception of credibility and homophily) matter in the news they produce, Gatekeeping Theory provides the theoretical framework to examine what other influences are also at play (Shoemaker and Vos, 2009). Therefore, the next paragraph sets out to contextualize the previous findings based on Gatekeeping Theory by first explaining the theoretical framework of gatekeeping.

Gatekeeping Theory

Since Kurt Lewin (1947) first coined the word *gatekeeping*, channel, forces, and gates have become metaphors to describe a process through which items become newsworthy or do not pass through the media gates (Shoemaker and Vos, 2009). Gatekeeping Theory has become an important framework to enhance understanding of what forces are important in shaping the news. For example, organizational rules may structure reporters' interactions with spokespersons as the programming of a news program provides deadlines and guidelines. Hence, Gatekeeping Theory explains the construction process of news content. By considering a variety of influences over news, Gatekeeping Theory provides the framework to interpret the results of this research and examine when journalists' perceptions matter in shaping the tone of the story.

The Underlying Assumption of Gatekeeping Theory

But before digging deep into the concept of gatekeeping, one important presumption of gatekeeping studies must be explained. Such an assumption remains under-discussed in the gatekeeping literature. The argument that "the mass media do not simply mirror the world around them" has deeper implications. The idea that mass media content is shaped, pounded, constrained, and encouraged by a multitude of forces (Shoemaker and Reese, 1996) suggests that such forces "create" a mediated reality and that they embody control over mediated reality, whereas other belief systems concerning the functions of the media may see control located in an event (Johnstone, Slawski, and Bowman, 1972). Shoemaker (1991) stated a constructive idea of gatekeeping explicitly when she wrote that gatekeepers provide a view of social reality, which includes the assumption that media organizations construct media reality from a particular viewpoint instead of describing reality as it is: "Gatekeeping is important because gatekeepers provide an integrated view of social reality to the rest of us…Gatekeeping is, therefore, a basic and powerful force in society" (p. 4). Gatekeeping empowers and transforms the media from being passive disseminators of news events into a powerful force that is as old as the process of communication. Gatekeeping dates back to the mid-1600s when "the town crier had to decide what to announce and what to withhold" (Shoemaker, 1991, p. 3). The following quote helps develop an understanding of a constructivist selectivity approach of gatekeeping:[2]

> The truth is that in our world the facts are infinitely many, and that no newspaper could print them all—even if they were fit to print—and nobody could read them. (Lippmann, 1999)

The question of whether media mirror or reconstruct reality has been debated for many years. Two arguments have been proposed: the first perspective argues that the media are a mirror of reality (i.e., Ptolemaic perspective) and are seen as passive transmitters, whereas in the second perspective, the media are selecting information and are active in the construction of reality (i.e., Copernican perspective; Burkart, 2002). Walter Lippmann (1999) pointed out that journalistic work is highly based on journalists' selective judgment of what is interesting, important, or both. Selection and interpretation are the basic tools of journalism. Such a perspective has a long tradition in the communication field and is also seen as the underlying assumption of this research. In accordance with Gatekeeping Theory, this research argues that mass media content remains a socially created product.

From "Mr. Gates" to Gatekeeping Theory

Gatekeeping Theory explains why news turns out the way it does. When Shoemaker and Reese (1991, 1996) published their book *Mediating the Message*, more discussion ensued on this topic among journalism scholars. However, theorizing about gatekeeping started long before that. Even though Kurt Lewin is known as the "father of gatekeeping," Leo C. Rosten (1937) is considered the first to carry out research on reporters. Funded by a fellowship from the Social Science Research Council of New York, Rosten investigated Washington correspondents for 16 months. He interviewed 127 journalists, wherein a majority of the correspondents felt inadequate to deal with economic issues. In their interviews, correspondents offered ample evidence that they were taken in by the unquestionable charm of President Franklin Delano Roosevelt's heroic manner and therefore felt that they had betrayed their objective roles, which they felt they must rigorously observe (Rosten, 1937). His empirical study showed evidence that the editorial stand influenced correspondents for many papers and that this situation could be frustrating for correspondents. One journalist said, "I'm sick of fighting my own office [...]. From now on I'm giving my paper what it wants" (Rosten, 1937, p. 51). Correspondents looked favorably on President Roosevelt because he was the first president to announce that correspondents can freely ask direct oral questions. Critics have claimed that President Roosevelt charmed the press and "prostituted" them to his end (Rosten, 1937). Rosten (1937) defined this period as "myth-making, myth-destroying," which started with this new journalistic process, the interpersonal relationship between politicians and reporters based on press conferences, and the exploration into the psychology of newspapermen.

Kurt Lewin is known as the "father of gatekeeping" because he was the first to pair the terms *gatekeeping* and *communication*. Thus, most of what is known today about the gatekeeping concept is derived from the field of psychology, when Lewin studied the changing food habits of a population. White (1950) summarized Kurt Lewin's influence as follows: "Before his untimely death, Dr. Lewin pointed out that the traveling of a news item through certain communication channels was dependent on the fact that certain areas within the channels functioned as 'gates'" (p. 383). In his unfinished manuscript "Frontiers in Group Dynamics II. Channels of Group Life; Social Planning and Action Research," Lewin (1947) developed field theory as a means to increase understanding of how to produce social change such as food habits in a population: "In the discussion of a social equilibrium it was emphasized that for understanding social events, and for planning social action, a reference from the phase space to the total social field is usually necessary" (p. 143).

A trained physicist, Lewin developed field theory to offer a way out of an ongoing battle in German psychology around World War I: Some psychologists were in favor of breaking down the person and the environment and studying them as isolated elements that could be causally connected. Lewin (1947), on the other hand, looked at a way to express such forces mathematically and was instead interested in the dynamics between those two elements—the person and the environment (Shoemaker, 1991). In his work, Lewin (1947) described how housewives played a particular role in determining food habits. Food comes to the family table through certain "channels." The most important channel is the grocery store. The force toward buying is composed of a number of components such as the buyer's own taste, his or her knowledge of the family's likes and dislikes, and his or her ideas about which goods are essential (Lewin, 1947). Another channel that carries food is the family garden.

The grocery and garden channels combine into the kitchen channel, where the food is stored either in the icebox or in the pantry. From there, the food comes to the table. The cook decides whether to cook the food or to pass it raw to the table. At each gate, food can be rejected or accepted, and the process of moving down the channel changes the food—potatoes can be fried or baked, vegetables cut up or not (Shoemaker and Vos, 2009).

According to Lewin (1947), gatekeeping involves a process of changes. And as Shoemaker and Vos (2009) noted, this means "changing [information] in ways to make them more appealing to the final consumer" (p. 13). The final decision to eat is further influenced by the colors of the food and their environmental context. The decisions of the gatekeepers depend partly on their ideology and their system of values and beliefs. Important in this theory of gatekeeping is the idea of forces that determine whether an item passes through a gate. Although channel, section, and gate all imply physical structures, it is clear that they all represent a process that describes why and how some items pass through a gate (Shoemaker and Vos, 2009). Lewin (1947) asserted that his theoretical framework could be applied generally. A good coincidence for mass communication science was that he shared a backyard fence with communication scholar Wilbur Schramm when both were at the University of Iowa. There, they hoed weeds and talked about theory (Shoemaker and Vos, 2009).

White (1950), a student of Wilbur Schramm, replicated Lewin's (1947) concept in a communications context. His input-output analysis observed the activities of one newswire editor of a small Midwestern newspaper who made news selection decisions based on his personal prejudices. White's purpose was to determine why one particular wire editor (whom he called "Mr. Gates") selected or rejected stories filed by three press associations. For one week, Mr. Gates saved every piece of wire copy he received. When his pages were filled, he went through the copies and specified the reason why he had rejected each story. He discovered that many of the rejected stories fell into the category of highly subjective value judgments. For example, Mr. Gates points out: "I have few prejudices, built in and otherwise, and there is little I can do about them. I dislike Truman's economics, daylight saving time and warm beer, but I go ahead using stories on them and other matters if I feel there is nothing more important to give space to" (White, 1950, p. 390). About one-third of the time, Mr. Gates rejected stories based on his personal evaluation of the content's merits (Shoemaker and Vos, 2009). Other reasons for rejection included lack of space or because similar news items had already been published. Another occurrence was that the later in the day the story came in, the higher was the proportion of his rejection due to lack of space (White, 1950). Although the analysis is descriptive with a normative bent and offers almost no predictive power, it remained a seminal piece of mass communication research. It initiated scholars to conduct similar research studies and led scholars to think about forces that shape news output. Gieber (1956), for example, expanded it to 16 wire editors for his doctoral work at the University of Wisconsin. He noted that the journalistic surroundings (e.g, work routines or deadlines) are just as important as the person who decides what passes through the gate.

Gates are decision points where items stop or move from one channel to another. The set of forces around a news gate forms a competitive environment, with positive and negative forces. Further thoughts on gatekeeping were influenced by more sophisticated explanations. Bass (1969) argued that White's study was in fact misplacing its focus by examining the telegraph editor, because he is not in a key decision position. Chibnall (1977) stated that the journalist-source relationship is the most important area of gatekeeping.

Shoemaker (1991) conceptualized a holistic model that acknowledges individual gatekeepers, internal and external forces, and feedback. The model recognizes effects from the individual level to the organizational, institutional, and societal levels. The main idea of Shoemaker's (1991) gatekeeping approach is that it classifies influences operating both separately and in linkage with each other. Shoemaker's (1991) model is an advancement of the Westley and MacLean (1957) model because she argued that at each step of the gatekeeping process, the selection tends to be heavily influenced by the anticipated selection criteria of the receiver. She further asserted that gatekeeping often involves more than one communication organization and that multiple acts of gatekeeping take place in a media organization (McQuail and Windhal, 1993). Shoemaker has greatly extended the simple news gatekeeping model, to account for the social system and the ideological and cultural contexts in which news gathering takes place. Figure 2.1 presents the impact that Shoemaker's (1991) publication has had on scholarly work in the sociology of news. To provide an argument on the impact of Shoemaker's (1991) work, all sociology of news studies (N = 362) in *Gatekeeping Theory* (Shoemaker and Vos, 2009) were coded that conducted research on gatekeeping processes. In essence, after Shoemaker and Reese (1991) published *Mediating the Message*, gatekeeping became a dominant paradigm (see figure 2.1). In 2009

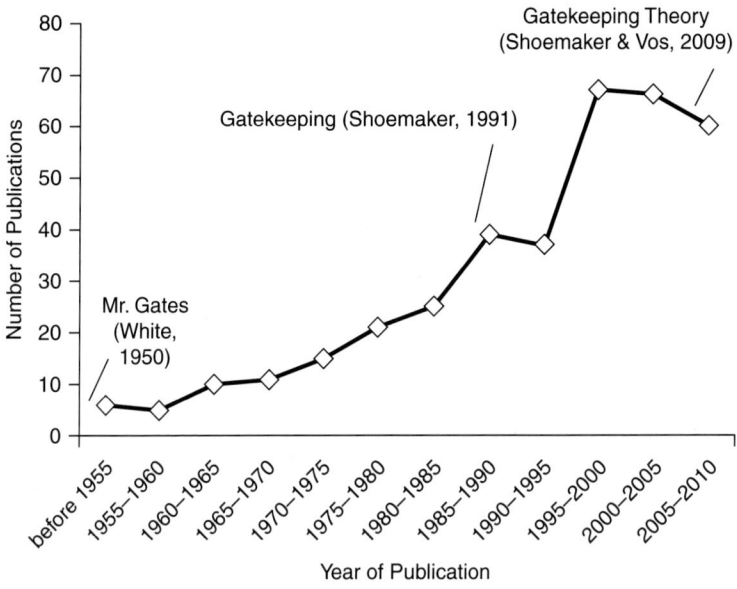

Figure 2.1 From "Mr. Gates" to Gatekeeping Theory (*N* = 362).

(Shoemaker and Vos, 2009), gatekeeping was coined *Gatekeeping Theory*. The next section provides an overview of what *Gatekeeping Theory* entails.

Gatekeeping: Levels of Analysis

According to Shoemaker and Vos (2009), "Gatekeeping Theory describes the process through which events are covered by the mass media, explains this process by considering concepts on five levels of analysis, and shows just how difficult it is to predict anything involving people" (p. 3). They applied five levels of analysis to the study of gatekeeping: the individual communication workers, the routines of communication work, the organizational level (e.g., media ownerships), the social institutional level (e.g., influences from government), and the social system level (e.g., cultural influences).

Research with a focus on individual gatekeepers looks at who gatekeepers are and how their personalities affect their news decisions. A variety of factors can be relevant to explain the individual level. For example, *ethnocentrism*, a term that describes the tendency of the mass media to frame and shape news events according to how well the news matches the national practices and values, has been found to be important for US journalists when they use their national values as the standard to evaluate all other countries (Shoemaker and Vos, 2009). Ethnocentrism is especially obvious when the topics are international news, mostly covering international relations. Furthermore, individualism affects the gatekeeping process insofar as it can be an important value to perceive sources. In the United States, for example, the media favorably present people who are self-actualized and self-sufficient and do not favorably present people who rely on others too much (Shoemaker and Vos, 2009). Moreover, individual gatekeepers are socialized and acculturated in a way that they take on historically articulated role conceptions and come to embrace culturally articulated values.

The routines level explains patterned practices that work to organize how journalists function in the social world. To analyze the routines level, mostly ethnographical studies were conducted that allowed the impact of these practices to be observed over time and in their natural setting (Reese, 2001; Reese and Ballinger, 2001; Reese and Lewis, 2009). The routine structuring of media also gives us an idea of how media organizations choose to deploy their resources. Routines emerge from three distinct sources that are known as journalists' orientation to the news-consuming audience, the external sources that journalists rely on for news, and the organizational culture and context in which news is created (Shoemaker and Vos, 2009).

The routines are the most immediate environment within which a journalist functions. On the other hand, the organizational level consists of imperatives, with which individuals are obliged to comply. An editorial policy, for example, allows the organization to decide what stories are newsworthy and how they are reported (Reese, 2001; Reese and Ballinger, 2001; Reese and Lewis, 2009). The routines and the organizational level are clearly related to each other. The ownership of the organizational network can be seen as a strong force over media content. Such organizational influence is not easily observed. As an example, the socialization process of new journalists into a news organization may be studied to understand organizational influence on how reporters adapt to specific editorial policies.

The social institution level of analysis, also conceptualized as the extra-media level (Reese, 2001), includes influencing factors outside the media institution. The power to shape the content is not the media's alone. Different institutions such as the government, public relations agencies, politicians, and other interest groups may have an impact on media content. Reese (2001) assumed that at this level, the media operate in structured relationships with other institutions that have the power to influence media content. Sources are important external influences and procedures that journalists use to identify and select. Journalists' need for credible information results in a dependence on well-elaborated sources. In a networked sourcing environment, extra-media influences have to be reconceptualized as an interactive and integrated part of media work. Sources may be an integrated part—and no longer an extra-media force—of a media organization. A reporter's network becomes integral to the work of journalism because of its nature of interconnectedness in a digitalized news environment. Participation, then, may emerge as a professional ethic of the journalism field, and distinctions between extra- and intra-media influences become blurred and are up for negotiation (Lewis, 2010).

The utmost level, the social-cultural level, is particularly important for this research: Are journalists in other countries working under the same constraints as US journalists? Some studies have shown that journalists of various countries tend to endorse the concept of press freedom and see news organizations as having a watchdog role over governments (Golding and Elliot, 1979; Logan and Kerns, 1985). Other studies have shown different results. For example, Galtung and Ruge (1965) argued that journalists' selection of information or news sources vary with their cultural backgrounds. Peterson (1979) found that foreign news selection was affected by different cultural backgrounds of journalists and concluded that homophily influences them in the sense that news from their own regions becomes more newsworthy. Cultural orientation predisposes journalists from Western countries to focus on events in which individual decisions are valued, whereas non-Western journalists prefer stories about collective decision making.

To date, Hanitzsch (2011) conducted the largest comparative study of journalism cultures around the world. In fact, the study surveyed 1,800 journalists in 18 countries. His research team crystallized the concept of journalism milieus, which are shared views on journalism's function in society. The journalistic field in Western countries is dominated by the detached watchdog milieu (journalists dedicated to objectivity and impartiality), whereas the opportunist facilitator (facilitator for political agenda) is the dominant milieu in developing, transitional, and authoritarian contexts (Hanitzsch, 2011). However, an empirical question remains: How do these milieus play out in the selection process of sources, for example? How do ideas of journalistic functions manifest themselves in practice, and under what conditions do they play out in what kind of a practical form?

Integrative Theories of Gatekeeping in Europe

While in the US tradition Shoemaker and Vos (2009) asserted that gatekeeping in a communication context can be studied on five levels, Donsbach (1987) conceptualized a gatekeeping model in the European context, which distinguishes between four spheres. In the first sphere, the *subject sphere*, Donsbach located values, norms, attitudes, and professional roles of journalists—factors that influence the journalist as an individual (Kunczik and Zipfel, 2001). The *professional sphere* entails social factors of journalists such as education, ethical principles, professional norms, news selection criteria, research methods, and social orientations. Furthermore, Donsbach argued that factors such as conditions of employment and internal press freedoms can be located in the third sphere, the *institutional sphere*. Within the *society sphere*, he located factors that influence the social surroundings of journalists, including relationships with sources; relationship with other journalists; public opinion; historical, regulatory, and political frameworks; and press freedoms (Kunczik and Zipfel, 2001). Weischenberg (1995), another German scholar, designed a similar model several years later. Weischenberg labeled the different levels of contexts and conceptualized an onion model, a frequent metaphor in social science to locate findings on micro, mezzo, and macro levels. The circles are set in a hierarchical order, and each level influences journalists. The inner layer is the media actor in its role context. Around this layer is the media statement, also known as the functional context in which effects and productivity of the journalism system are located. The next circle entails the media institution, the structural context such as conditions and necessities of the institution where the journalist works. The outermost circle is the media system or the norm context.

Only a few differences exist between Weischenberg's (1995) and Donsbach's (1987) concept: Weischenberg conceptualized a hierarchical model, whereas Donsbach conceptualized all four spheres as equal in terms of power of influence. Second, Weischenberg located professionalism and socialization on the role context, whereas Donsbach located it on the professional sphere. Third, Donsbach located professional and ethical standards in the professional sphere, whereas Weischenberg located it in the norm context. Frank Esser (1998) later investigated how the different factors influence one another and how the different contexts (i.e., Weischenberg) or spheres (i.e., Donsbach) are linked to one another. He distinguished four spheres to explain factors that influence journalism: the subject sphere, the institutional sphere, the media structural sphere, and the society sphere. He pointed out that it is not always possible to locate one factor to a sphere. For example, ethics are important on all four spheres. Ten years later, Donsbach (2008a) outlined four levels where independent variables can be located that influence the news-selection process. His reverse pyramid explained that predictability advances with each level downward. It reaches its maximum on the individual level; it is much harder to predict behavior if conducting research on a higher level than the individual because then the research has to consider all the intervening variables (Donsbach, 2008a).

However, only Shoemaker (1991) and Shoemaker and Vos (2009) conceptualized gatekeeping as a process model. That is important, because news judgment is a process within a larger field as stated by Lewin (1947). Donsbach (2004) held that most of the current models or theories of journalists' news decisions concentrate on news factors and do not explain the underlying processes leading to news judgment. This is surprising, as one of the earliest communication models by Westley and MacLean (1957) focused on cognitive-psychological factors in the communication process.

Another aspect relevant to future theorizing of gatekeeping as the selection process of credible sources is to think about links between influences from individual, routine, and organizational levels, for example. What does it imply if "the more media workers follow the routines of their organizations, the more likely their content is to be used" (Shoemaker and Reese, 1996, p. 267) or that "the personal attitudes and values of news media owners may be reflected not only in editorials and columns but also in news and features" (Shoemaker and Reese, 1996, p. 267)? Or what influence does organization size have on the frames of sources in news content if "chain organizations are more likely to endorse presidential candidates than independent organizations, and the endorsement is generally homogeneous throughout the chain" (Shoemaker and Reese, 1996, p. 268)?

What Remains of Gatekeeping Theory?

In journalism sociology, scholars studying the process of how news gets selected and (re-)constructed cannot ignore Gatekeeping Theory if they strive to gain a holistic overview of why news turns out the way it does. Thus, Gatekeeping Theory has long influenced our explanations of how news is framed. Hanitzsch (2007b) has argued that Gatekeeping Theory is not a theory on its own. If theories are sets of statements that are interrelated; logically consistent; and describe, explain, and predict some portion of reality (Shoemaker et al., 2004), Gatekeeping Theory can indeed be considered a theory of sociology of news—at least from a normative standpoint. To understand a variety of mechanisms involved in the practical tasks of journalism, Gatekeeping Theory provides a heuristic framework describing what forces might be at play when journalists work in the newsroom. With that said, it remains an empirical question whether these forces indeed affect newsmakers, whether they are perceived as such forces by journalists or editors themselves, and whether they are structured in a hierarchical order. Indeed, there are studies that hint at the assumption of a hierarchical structure in journalism (Hanitzsch and Mellado, 2011). However, such assumptions still require empirical investigations of what portion of reality (Shoemaker et al., 2004) and what portion of news they predict to account for theories of news. It further remains an empirical question if journalists are aware of gatekeeping forces or if such forces work as part of an illusive system that does not enable them to understand forces beyond the newsroom. In other words, influences from outside the newsroom might be less immediate and therefore less likely to be perceived as a restricting force because such forces are not directly part of journalists' everyday experiences.

Furthermore, some journalism scholars argue that the news media stand at a juncture where journalists' gatekeeping role is changing (Bruns, 2005)—that is, Gatekeeping Theory is in transition and the outcome is yet unknown. Because the dominant news-funding model is collapsing (Kawamoto, 2003) and the news media face a crisis of trust (Gans, 2003), the role of journalists as gatekeepers has to be met with new skepticism. On the other hand, Benson (2004) has cautioned that a debate on what the media actually are has been delayed for many years. Benson (2004) argued that to better understand what the media are, it is necessary to study the process and not just attribute new factors to certain news outcomes. In fact, media sociologists have long called for visualizing such "seemingly self-evident" structured structures that play out in practice (e.g., Bourdieu, 1998b; Darnton, 1975; Schultz, 2007).

Critical Issues of Gatekeeping

The main purpose of Lewin's (1947) seminal piece was to outline basic characteristics of a field theory, complementary to White's (1950) adaption of the theory to the media context. The field is the complex environment in which a phenomenon occurs. While the individual is still at the center of the theory for Lewin, due to his background in psychology, field theory today broadly investigates how societal macrostructures are linked to organizational routines and practices. Shoemaker and Vos (2009) argued that Benson (2006) offered a great contribution to the field, outlining how journalistic fields vary across social systems and cultures. Benson (2006) analyzed what French sociologist Pierre Bourdieu added to the concept of news media as a journalistic field. Bourdieu (1979, 1984) located the journalistic field within a field of power, caught between cultural and economic power. Individual decisions are limited by those macrostructures (i.e., cultural and economic power), organizational routines, and journalistic practices.

Linear thinking processes have influenced much contemporary thinking about gatekeeping. This process can best be described as examining a relationship between two concepts or two variables. Such examples are very common in gatekeeping research; linear statements include, "Events are more likely to be covered than issues" (Shoemaker and Reese, 1996, p. 266) or "Journalists' role conceptions affect content" (Shoemaker and Reese, 1996, p. 264). Nevertheless, Shoemaker and Reese (1996) concluded that an important step in gatekeeping is "synthesizing what is known about influences on media content into a more systematic set of interrelated statements about the relationships between media content and the influences on it—a theory" (p. 261). However, as Bourdieu (1984) has cautioned, "to account for infinite diversity of practices in a way that is both unitary and specific, one has to break with linear thinking" (p. 105). If attributing a news report as an outcome of one level of analysis, one formulates a rule that fits the observed regularity in a purely descriptive way. Such a determining cause of the practice neglects the mechanism through which the relationship is established between the structures and practices or news representations (Bourdieu, 1977). For example, how journalists are socialized or how journalistic resources (i.e., who covers which story, whose story makes the front page) are distributed present important social influences on how stories turn out the way they do.

The idea of journalistic fields helps ground cultural analyses and can explain under-theorized aspects of news production. In particular, the idea of a journalistic field sets a theoretical framework to understand changes and dynamics in the journalistic field, in which Gatekeeping Theory falls short in outlining these forces that stand in stark contrast to each other and are part of journalists' struggle to meet the expectations of performing a normative role by focusing on forces that shape the news. Shoemaker and Vos (2009) acknowledged that shortcoming when they wrote, "Regrettably, theorizing about gatekeeping has not been in large supply" (p. 11). In a digitalized world of information overflow, where news is distributed with speed like never before, such an undertaking seems fundamental to better understand why the news turns out the way it does. The profession of journalism is losing its control, and the traditional financial model is collapsing. Journalists are laid off or become aggregators at a time when their professional news filters are crucial to help people successfully navigate their lives in an increasingly complex world. However, even though globalization is mostly understood as Americanization, other countries remain surprisingly resistant against influences from the United States.

For example, western European countries have adopted market-model journalism to some extent (e.g., increasing their market orientation in tabloid newspapers) but remain path dependent in envisioning the function of media as social institutions (i.e., the BBC model in the United Kingdom). Hallin and Mancini (2004) provided empirical evidence that different philosophies have led to different concepts of media systems: western European countries have long been skeptical of a free media market and seek to improve diversity of media content by assigning a specific role to the state as a regulative force to enhance the media's role as a social institution.

Because this study looks at Washington correspondents from various countries, such differences are crucial to the understanding of differences in journalism cultures. Levels of analysis are important models to structure dimensions of analysis; they serve a heuristic potential but explain practice in a deterministic logic by arguing that social systems exert influence over news content, whereas social systems structure journalists' practices and not news content. Structural influences such as organizational constraints, editors' guidance, profit expectations of the news organization, and audience expectations provide a structure to journalists' profession. But the news content is a product of journalists' practice based on these structural constraints.

Hanitzsch, Altmeppen, and Schlueter (2007) stated in *Journalism Theories of the Next Generation* that levels of influence are often used in communication research because they are not conceptually complex. They outlined new sociological frameworks and proposed theoretical innovations on how to study the sociology of news to enhance our understanding of global and local trends in the profession of journalism. The scholars' attempts are by no means to break with the older generation but rather to approach journalism studies from concepts that have not been very well established, such as field, habitus, milieu, and power. Although journalism research in Germany has been highly influenced by terms related to system theory and has greatly contributed to the heuristic inquiries of journalism as a scientific field, it has left empirical gaps between scientific knowledge and practical relevance.

Another challenge that the new generation highlights is a search to more firmly establish the boundaries of the journalism field. On one hand, new entrants such as news bloggers (e.g., iReporters at CNN) demand a greater tolerance and openness of journalism as an institution. On the other hand, journalism is a form of public communication legitimized as a social institution that advocates for society. If everyone is perceived to be a journalist, then normative and democratic claims can no longer be targeted toward journalism as an institution, but the responsibility would be a collective responsibility. In other words, society could no longer hold news organizations responsible for not fulfilling a democratic function and the news media trust issue would eventually become a serious crisis, especially in democracies. To conclude, in a search to establish the boundaries of journalism from other fields, it is crucial to conceptualize journalism as a practice so that journalists can be held responsible for what they practice.

The most recent paradigm in comparative journalism research— *The West and the Global*—focuses on this exact paradoxical coexistence: in the universal and the specific in journalism cultures around the world (Wahl-Jorgensen and Hanitzsch, 2009). A paradigm shift has recently emerged because of methodological concerns that national borders may not necessarily correspond to divisions based on cultural, linguistic, and ethnic criteria. News production may still be geared toward a domestic audience (Wahl-Jorgensen and Hanitzsch, 2009). However, with normative claims of multiculturalism, the concept of a domestic audience may also have shifted toward a multicultural domestic audience as well as new media outlets entering the market that target a transnational audience (such as Al-Jazeera). The internet enables domestic journalism to act as an international distributor. Furthermore, cross-border regions (e.g., regions with a high number of diverse cultures) increasingly enjoy attention from scholars and practitioners. Brussels, as the headquarters of the European Union, as well as Washington, DC, as headquarters of foreign correspondents, are examples of cross-border regions. In such cases, national borders may not correspond to a common sense of identity. National borders are blurred by a coexistence of diverse cultures because the same culture may not exist in just one nation. Interaction patterns between cultures become an important aspect of practical and empirical concerns; culture is expressed over its relative component and manifests itself in such interactions. Such an inquiry moves the paradigm of the universal and the specific toward an intercultural paradigm in comparative research as a way to study journalism as a multicultural field through its interactions and relationships with diverse sources. It provides an understanding of how the universal and the specific, which are set in relation to other cultures, frame interactions and eventually affect media messages.

Gatekeeping Theory fails to consider that news organizations embody a particular history that defines their position in the journalism field, which limits their actions and defines their amount of cultural, economic, and social capital (i.e., their resources). In other words, organizations' cultures vary according to their position, and comparing them without taking into account their field position limits comparability. By putting journalists in relation to other fields, field position can be integrated into the analysis to shed light on news production and forces that structure news decisions. Extra-media level influences that are other fields (e.g., the political or economic field) then structure journalism in a way that sets the framework for its professional task. In a journalism context, the field metaphor refers to the idea that powerful poles attempt to pull journalism's resources in their direction to increase the prominence of their position in their own field and pull away resources from the journalism field. Such an example includes politicians setting ground rules for media organizations on how to quote government officials. Eventually, strategically framing media messages may well enhance public perceptions and re-election chances of politicians (i.e., exerting power over the journalism field by setting the rules). In that situation, it may well be that pulling resources from one field increases resources and autonomy in another field. In any case, the dependency of various fields is most important in understanding a social field logic: various forces are at work, which attempt to convert parts of their capital to establish a dominant position in their field.

For example, if journalists are influenced by advertisers to cover a story in a certain way, such circumstances may pull the news organization's position toward the economic pole because of its immediate dependence on transparent success, and there may exist an implicit expectation to satisfy the demands of advertisers. If news organizations can resist such a force, then they can play their cultural capital card (i.e., invested cultural capital).

Field as a metaphor implies the structure of a social space. According to Bourdieu (1998b), social spaces or social classes are never studied in and for themselves but are instead tested through research in which the theoretical and the empirical are inseparable and which mobilizes numerous methods of observations and measurements—quantitative and qualitative. Bourdieu (1998b) argued that the "deepest logic of the social world can be grasped only if one plunges into the particularity of an empirical reality, historically located and dated, but with the objective of constructing it as a special case of what is possible" (p. 2). Even if a deterministic logic exists within a historically located empirical reality, journalism practice does not in every case follow such a logic because history sets the framework of what is possible.

The closer agents are to each other, the more they have in common. To each class of position corresponds a class of habitus (or tastes) produced by social conditioning (i.e., an affinity of style or a habitus, according to a journalist's position in the social field). As Bourdieu (1998b) stated, "Habitus are generative principles of distinct and distinctive practices—what the worker eats, and especially the way he eats, the sport he practices and the way he practices, his political opinion" (p. 8).

Journalistic Field Logic

Bourdieu argued that the field of journalism is part of the field of cultural production and part of the field of power (Benson, 2006). Even though the journalistic field is a weak autonomous field (e.g., dependent on the rules of the economic field), what is happening in the field can be best understood by examining the degree of autonomy of the field. Benson (2006) conceptualized the journalistic field and the newsroom as hierarchical social spaces where journalistic capital defines autonomy within the field. The journalistic capital can be observed by autonomy in the journalistic field, absence of economic influences on the media organization, and independence from advertising. The journalistic capital is high where the economic capital is low. For the purpose of this research, journalistic capital is conceptualized as Bourdieu's (1986) original conceptualization of cultural capital. The different forms of cultural capital that reporters hold within the field of journalism may explain why some individual characteristics may influence the gatekeeping process whereas individual characteristics of another reporter may not influence the gatekeeping process at all.

The journalistic field is structured along the two poles: between journalists who are independent of political and economic power and those who are dependent on these commercial powers. In a recent study that compared journalistic milieus in 18 countries, Hanitzsch (2011) argued that three factors play out in the journalistic field: professional autonomy, commercial and political influence, and ownership. Results examined journalists in the detached watchdog milieu; journalists define their role as skeptical and critical agents, watching government elites. Most of the time, journalists who focus on providing the audience with political information experience the highest degree of autonomy, both in terms of having control over their work and in taking part in decisions that affect their work. According to Hanitzsch (2011), journalists in Germany showed the highest agreement toward the detached watchdog milieu, as journalists belonging to this milieu were mostly found in publicly owned media and Germany has a strong public service broadcasting institution. Journalists who report on politicians are assumed to have higher levels of journalistic autonomy than other journalists (Hanitzsch, 2011).

Research shows a negative relationship between professional autonomy and perceived influences from economic and external forces such as political sources or advertisers. That is, weak external influences will result in higher autonomy. Journalists might be more vulnerable to their social position and their personal resources of cultural and economic capital if heteronomous agents do not "direct" their positions. If journalists' work is less structured by external influences, then their positions in the field (i.e., their cultural capital) become more of a structuring force of their choices and behavior. To summarize, correspondents' perceptions and interactions are more likely to shape news content and expression of cultural capital if heteronomous forces such as economic constraints, advertising influences, and ownership guidelines do not influence their reporting.

Notes

1. From the total sample of foreign correspondents, 33.3 percent came from western Europe, 14.6 percent from northern Europe, 10.6 percent from eastern Europe, 9.3 percent from eastern Asia, 8 percent from western Asia, 6.6 percent from Canada, 6.6 percent from South America, 4 percent from central America, 4 percent from southern Asia, and 2.6 percent from southern Europe.
2. A more in-depth discussion on media reality paradigms can be found in Bentele, 2008.

3

News-Gathering and Sourcing Routines of DC Correspondents

I still think that, like in any professional relationship, technologies can definitely help a great deal, but at the end, the personal/face-to-face relationship is still the most valuable and useful.

—Foreign correspondent, personal communication,
Washington, DC, January 2012

Journalists' perceptions are structured by their routines and their interactions with sources. Information is gathered through various means of communication, each contributing to the amount and content of information available in a news report. As discussed previously, foreign correspondents interact less frequently with US sources over the phone and instead tend to gather information from other media. Hence, the question remains how these structuring principles of the news-gathering process affect journalists' perceptions of politicians. What is the quality distinction between personal contacts and information gathered from websites?

Personal Contact

According to Willnat and Weaver's (2003) analysis of foreign correspondents, access to US sources was the greatest challenge for foreign correspondents in Washington, DC. Face-to-face interactions and other personal forms of communication can be important for categorizing a source as a person belonging to the in-group or the out-group (Ho and McLeod, 2008). People experience more social presence in face-to-face communication settings and exchange more information (i.e., talk more) than in computer-mediated settings. The idea of being aware of someone's field position enhances journalists' own understanding of their positions.

Social presence has not been researched in a journalism context. The working environment may influence the extent of the influence of one variable on the other (perceived homophily influence on source credibility), but if a theory is robust, it should not lead to a nonexistent relationship. Journalists' high amount of professional freedom when gathering news exclusively and in a personal setting has been documented by studies showing that when journalists have a high amount of autonomy, they are more likely to have control over their work (Hanitzsch, 2011; Hanitzsch et al., 2011). In addition, higher amounts of social presence in personal interviews may contribute to a higher amount of journalists' perceptions showing up in their reporting. That is, if journalists have more autonomy, their perceptions are more likely to influence the stories they report.

To test the relationship between routines of interactions and perception, the amount of access to political sources for their last news stories was included in the analysis. Results show that journalists high on background homophily ($M = 30.52$, $SD = 6.04$) perceive sources as more trustworthy than journalists low on background homophily ($M = 27.09$, $SD = 5.28$) if they had personal contact with their sources (for tests of significance, see table 3.1).

Table 3.1   News-Gathering Group Differences

	Competence	Trustworthiness	Goodwill
In-Person			
Background Homophily (low)	31.77 (4.94)	27.09 (5.28)**	27.53 (5.48)
Background Homophily (high)	32.09 (6.43)	30.51 (6.03)**	28.76 (6.19)
Attitude Homophily (low)	28.72 (4.90)**	26.08 (4.90)**	26.48 (5.50)*
Attitude Homophily (high)	34.75 (5.56)**	31.46 (6.33)**	29.64 (5.98)*
No Personal Contact			
Background Homophily (low)	32.85 (4.75)	28.38 (4.43)	27.28 (4.16)
Background Homophily (high)	31.64 (4.25)	28.63 (3.84)	28.72 (3.96)
Attitude Homophily (low)	32.16 (5.13)	28.16 (3.76)	27.05 (4.54)
Attitude Homophily (high)	32.71 (4.86)	29.05 (5.20)	29.21 (4.48)

Note: One-way ANOVA
*Significant at the .05 level.
** Significant at the .001 level.

An interesting finding was that perceptions of attitude homophily were a significant predictor for all three dimensions of source credibility—competence, trustworthiness, and goodwill—for journalists who had personal contact with their sources. However, no significant effect was found for correspondents who perceived their sources to be homophilous but who had no personal contact with their sources.

Indeed, perceptual differences manifested themselves through personal contact and in-person interviews. Hence, perceived homophily contributed the most to perceptions of source credibility when personal contact was used as a news-gathering method.

Sourcing Dimension: Personal Contact Matters for Perception

Once journalists meet a political source in person, their perception of the source's credibility is influenced by similarities of values. Without personal contact, such perceptions have a smaller impact. Higher amounts of social presence in personal interviews may contribute to a higher amount of autonomy because journalists are "on the ground" and hence their perceptions might be more likely to influence the stories they report as they become experts on site and thus become unique channels of information gathering.

News Gathering from Other Media: The Extra-Media Level of Influence

Foreign journalists in DC depend significantly more on other media's reporting when gathering news, so in what way does dependency on other media affect journalists' perceptions of politicians' source credibility? This study shows that journalists who do not quote other media and perceive low background homophily with their sources ($M = 26.95, SD = 3.90$) perceive politicians as less caring about their audience than journalists who do not consult other media and perceive high background homophily ($M = 28.90, SD = 5.59$). In other words, personal contact and the perception of sharing similar values positively influence the journalists' perception of a politician's goodwill and trustworthiness.

Figure 3.1 shows how quoting other media influences the relationship between journalists' background homophily and their perception

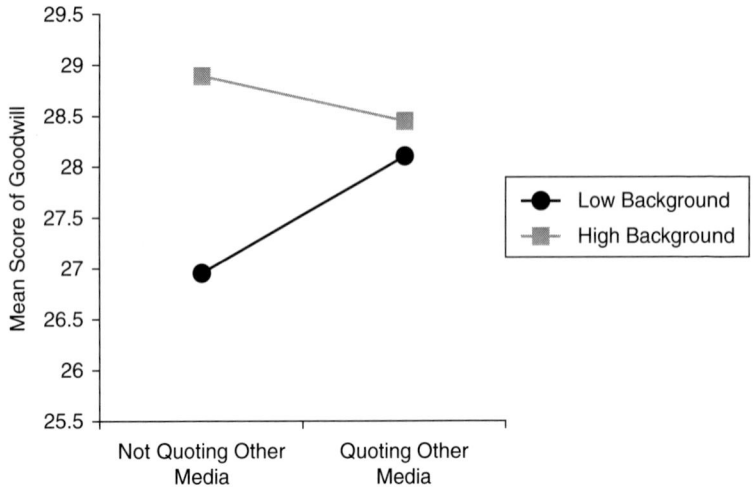

Figure 3.1 Correspondents' Perception of Goodwill, Based on Homophily and Quoting of Other Media.

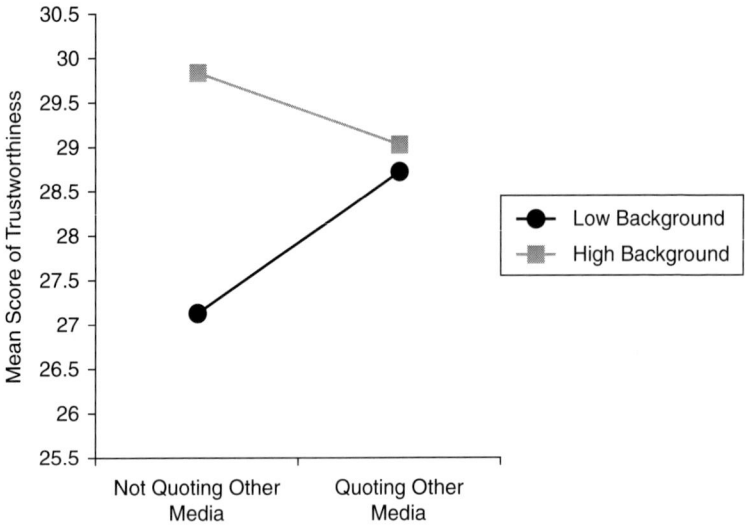

Figure 3.2 Correspondents' Perception of Trustworthiness, Based on Homophily and Quoting of Other Media.

Note: Perceptions of goodwill and trustworthiness were measured on a six-item scale (7-point semantic differential items). The numbers in this figure represent the means of the total scores of the goodwill and trustworthiness items.

of politicians' goodwill. If journalists quote other media, then their own backgrounds do not influence their perceptions of goodwill. However, if they rely less on other media and do not quote them in their reporting, their perceptions of politicians' backgrounds influence their perceptions of politicians' goodwill. If they perceive politicians to share a similar background, then they perceive them to be more caring about the public. If they perceive them to have a dissimilar background, they perceive them as significantly less caring about the public. The same dynamic was found for the trustworthiness dimension: if journalists did not quote other media and perceived politicians as similar to them, they would perceive them as being more trustworthy as well (also see figure 3.2).

Social Media and Perceptual Forces

For the perception of politicians having goodwill, correspondents who gathered information from social media ($M = 26.90$, $SD = 5.13$) perceived politicians as having less goodwill compared to correspondents who did not gather information from social media ($M = 28.10$, $SD = 4.90$) / ($F(1,147) = 4.23, p < .05$). Furthermore, the same dynamic emerged for correspondents' perception of trustworthiness: correspondents who consulted an official website ($M = 27.10$, $SD = 3.38$) or attended an official press conference ($M = 27.41$, $SD = 3.93$) significantly perceived their sources as less trustworthy ($F(1,147) = 5.68$, $p < .02$) and ($F(1,147) = 4.16$, $p < .05$), respectively, than correspondents who did not attend a press conference ($M = 29.47$, $SD = 5.41$) or correspondents who did not consult an official website ($M = 29.19$, $SD = 5.33$).

Sourcing Dimension: Social Media Decrease Trustworthiness and Goodwill

These findings point out that that we might still see the personal interview and personal access as the most credible interaction with sources, and hence, sourcing materials from social media might be considered less credible than personal contacts. This shows that social media have not replaced personal contact as a major source of information in DC.

Journalists' Autonomy and the Influence of Perceptions

A large body of literature examines role conceptions or professional worldviews to better understand what journalists' autonomy entails: Which normative roles (e.g., the disseminator, the investigator, the adversarial, and the mobilizer role) do journalists follow to perform their job (Weaver at al., 2007)? Role conception has been defined as journalists' perception of journalism's social functions in society (Donsbach, 2008b; Weaver et al., 2007). Those perceived social functions are assumed to shape the stories that journalists ultimately report. The comparative perspective suggests that the extent to which journalists identify with a particular role or function varies across cultures and in its relations to heteronomous pressures, initial formation, and subsequent historical trajectory of the field (Hanitzsch, 2011). However, what happens if journalists are more likely to be exposed to ideas of a particular kind of cosmopolitan journalism, which may conflict with heteronomous pressures on their work (i.e., Reese, 2001)? In a previous study with the same data set, the disseminator role (which conceptually reflects the idea of the detached watchdog but was renamed according to Weaver et al., 2007) was the most embraced role by both US and foreign journalists in Washington, DC (Tandoc, Hellmueller, and Vos, 2013). The disseminator role was perceived to be the most important role conception ($M = 4.39$, $SD = .65$), followed by the investigator role ($M = 4.30$, $SD = .56$), the adversarial role ($M = 3.07$, $SD = 1.02$), and the mobilizer role ($M = 2.78$, $SD = .98$). The disseminator role consists of five items for this research: "It's my job to be impartial," "Objectivity is a goal that I strive for," "It's my job to lay out all relevant sides of an issue," "I attempt to fairly express the position of each side in a political debate," and "I try to suspend my political preferences when working on news stories."

Because the disseminator role was perceived to be the most important role, this role was tested in relationship with perceived homophily and source credibility to see how the idea of the disseminator conflicts with the perception of credibility and homophily.

Results revealed that journalists who embrace the disseminator role and perceive low attitude homophily with their sources ($M = 28.61$, $SD = 6.56$) perceive their sources as less competent in spite of the disseminator role they embrace. On the other hand, journalists who embrace the disseminator role and perceive high attitude homophily ($M = 34.65$, $SD = 5.59$) evaluate their source as more competent ($F(1,58) = 14.683$,

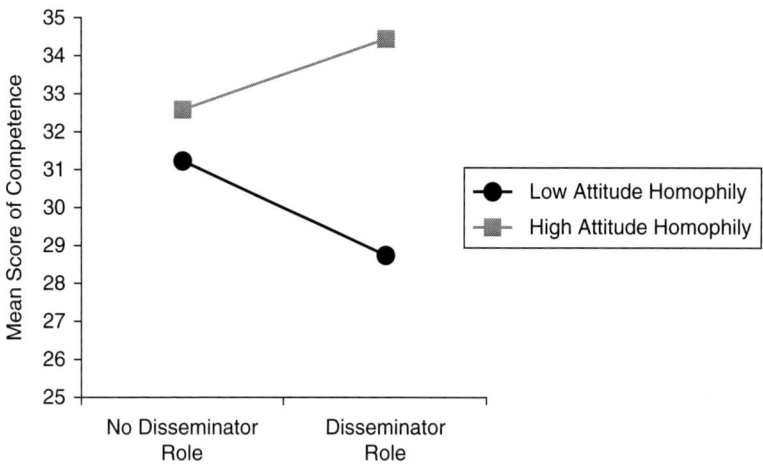

Figure 3.3 Correspondents' Perception of Competence, Based on Homophily and the Disseminator Role.

$p < .0001$). One reason the perception of similarity positively influences perceptions of credibility may be that the role is mainly a professional variable, whereas the perception of similarity is a rather subjective variable. It might well be that perception becomes more important when journalists believe they should follow the disseminator role very strictly so that they follow the ethical guidelines of journalism.

Figure 3.3 shows that if correspondents embrace a disseminator role and perceive politicians to share similar attitudes, they are significantly more likely to perceive politicians as competent sources. If correspondents embrace a disseminator role and perceive politicians to share a dissimilar background, they are significantly less likely to perceive politicians as competent. However, if journalists do not embrace a disseminator role, journalists' perceptions of politicians' attitudes are not related to their perceptions of politicians' competence.

However, the study further revealed that journalists who embrace the disseminator role and perceive low attitude homophily with their sources ($M = 25.27$, $SD = 4.13$) are significantly less likely to perceive their sources to be trustworthy than journalists who embrace the disseminator role and perceive high attitude homophily ($M = 30.95$, $SD = 6.19$) in how they evaluate the trustworthiness dimension ($F(1,58) = 14.56$, $p < .001$); see figure 3.4.

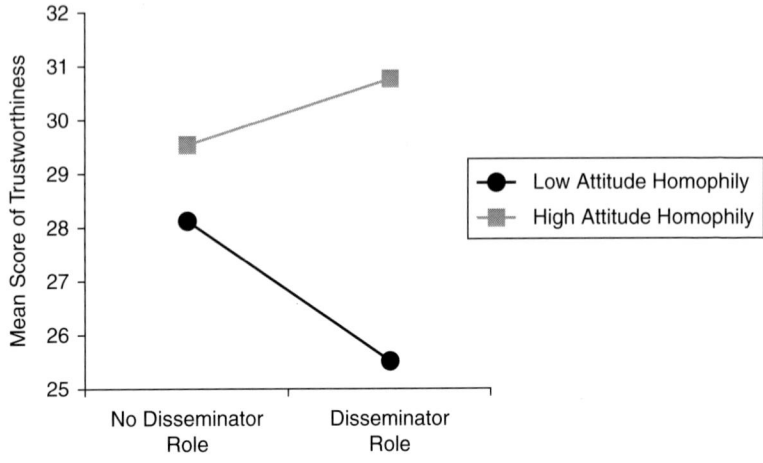

Figure 3.4   Correspondents' Perception of Trustworthiness, Based on Homophily and the Disseminator Role.

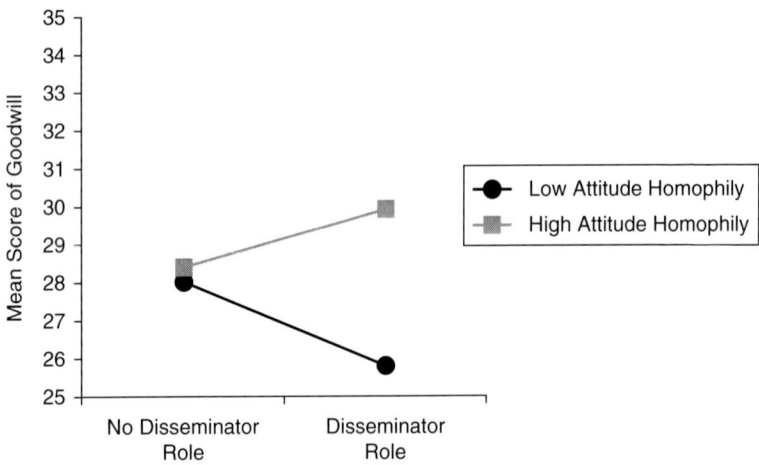

Figure 3.5   Correspondents' Perception of Goodwill, Based on Homophily and the Disseminator Role.

Figure 3.4 reveals that if correspondents perceive politicians to share their values and have similar thoughts and ideas, they are more likely to perceive politicians as trustworthy if correspondents embrace the disseminator role. If correspondents perceive politicians as not sharing their values, they are less likely to perceive them as trustworthy sources if journalists embrace the disseminator role. If journalists do not embrace the disseminator role, their perceptions of politicians' attitudes are not predicting journalists' perceptions of sources' trustworthiness.

In addition, the same holds true for the goodwill dimension: journalists who embrace the disseminator role and perceive low attitude homophily with their sources ($M = 25.79$, $SD = 5.61$) are significantly different from journalists who embrace the disseminator role and perceive high attitude homophily ($M = 29.95$, $SD = 5.54$) in how they evaluate the goodwill dimension ($F(1,58) = 8.28$, $p < .006$); see figure 3.5.

Correspondents who embrace the disseminator role and perceive politicians as treating people as they would like to be treated and perceive politicians as sharing their values are more likely to perceive such sources as embodying goodwill (i.e., caring about their public). However, correspondents who embrace the disseminator role and perceive politicians as not sharing their same ideas and thoughts are significantly less likely to perceive politicians as caring about their public.

Sourcing Dimension: Role Conception Matters for Perceptions of Sources

Perceived homophily will produce more positive perceptions of source credibility, only to the extent that journalists embrace the disseminator role. However, this was fully supported for the attitude homophily dimension but not for the background homophily dimension.

Do Perceptions Matter for the News Journalists Produce?

Some journalism scholars have argued that journalists' attitudes are evident in their reporting (Graber, 2002; Patterson and Donsbach, 1996; Starck and Soloski, 1977). However, such a claim remains an untested assumption. This study tests the assumption with self-reported data of the same correspondents but frames the question as "how your news organization portrayed the source" to account for social desirability as one major validity problem of surveys. To ensure that a variety of sources were included as sources of the correspondents' last news story, an open-ended question first asked the correspondents to briefly describe their last news story without explicitly mentioning their sources. Four examples (randomly chosen) are listed in table 3.2.

Table 3.2   Examples of Correspondents' Most Recent Source Interaction

Story on US and European sanctions on Syria.
House committee's decision to increase disaster relief funds by taking back funds committed for loans for advanced vehicle technology.
An analysis of President Barack Obama's Middle East speech and his meeting with Israeli Prime Minister Benjamin Netanyahu at the White House.
Press Conference State Department Hillary Clinton and Austrian Secretary of State Michael Spindelegger.

The regression analysis helped to reveal whether perceptions matter for news content. The purpose of regression was to test whether a set of predictors changes the variance explained. In the following example, the F value changes significantly if the source credibility block is entered after the homophily block. Hence, the homophily block ($F(3,148) = 3.226$, $p < .03$) in combination with the source credibility block ($F(3,148) = 3.879$, $p < .001$) represents the best predictor model of source valence in news reports. In fact, background homophily ($\beta = 1.024$, $t = 2.304$, $p < .05$) and goodwill ($\beta = .126$, $t = 2.173$, $p < .05$) were both significant and positive predictors of source valence in news stories (see table 3.3).

To summarize, it was assumed that the higher the perceived source credibility, the more positive the media's representation of that politician. This hypothesis was partially supported. Goodwill was a significant predictor of valence. Also, background homophily significantly predicted source valence in news stories.

Sourcing Dimension: Perceived goodwill and background homophily lead to more positive coverage of political sources.

Perceived Autonomy

Without doubt, journalists do not always have the autonomy to decide on the content or the tone of a news story. To have a clearer idea of when perception matters for the news journalists produce and when not, perceived autonomy was also taken into account.

It was assumed that journalists' perception of source credibility would produce a positive valence of a political source in their stories if they enjoyed high autonomy at work. And the same dynamic was assumed for the perception of similarity that journalists' perception

Table 3.3   Predicting Source Valence in News Stories

	β	T
Demographics		
Gender	–.100	.228
Origin	–.512	–1.172
Homophily		
Attitude	.539	–1.113
Background	1.024	2.304*
Competence	.072	1.471
Source Credibility		
Trustworthiness	.000	.003
Goodwill	.126	2.173*

Note: $F(7,148) = 3.462$, $p < .003$; $R = .383$; $R^2 = .147$.
* Significant at the .05 level.
** Significant at the .001 level.

would only matter for their reporting if they are autonomous in deciding how to cover their sources.

Because the research was based on survey responses, autonomy was conceptualized as perceived autonomy. To assess perceived autonomy, there were two methods used. First, correspondents rated how much influence each level (i.e., individual-level factors, routine factors, organizational factors) should have on their work. Then they rated the same level of influences on how much these levels influenced their most recent news story. With such a procedure, autonomy was first assessed from within the field and then looked at by their practice (i.e., their last news story). Hence, an attempt was made to achieve an understanding of autonomy as how it ought to be and was measured on a normative level and how it played out in their last news story. Such a procedure does not take into account individual differences of perceived autonomy based on different journalism cultures but provides an overall understanding of how professional autonomy can be conceptualized.[1]

The analysis revealed three distinctive factors of influence for the last news story as well as for the normative-phrased items. The first dimension of influence over correspondents' work was the individual level, which is the influence of a foregoing interaction with a political source as well as correspondents' own experiences with a political source. The second dimension refers to the routine level, which includes influence from news deadlines, journalists' in-groups (colleagues), supervisor or higher editor, and feedback from audiences.

Table 3.4   Correlation Matrix of Level of Influence (Normative Factors)

	Individual	Routine	Organizational
Individual Level	—	.23*	.02
Routine Level	.23*	—	.20*
Organizational Level	.02	.20*	—

* Significant at the .05 level.
** Significant at the .001 level.

An implied causal relationship was tested for the normative-phrased question: the organizational level correlated highest with the routine level of influence ($r = .20$, $p < .05$), and the individual level correlated highest with routine processes ($r = .23$, $p < .05$). As a result, the routine level correlated high with both the organizational level and the individual level of influence (see table 3.4).

The findings point out that the two groups (US and foreign correspondents) are similar in their understanding of how much influence each of the three levels of influence should have on their work. The three levels of influence appeared in the same ranking order for the two groups, with the individual level showing the highest agreement. The individual level was perceived as "should have some influence" (US: $M = 3.04$, $SD = .98$; Foreign: $M = 3.05$, $SD = .98$). Second, the routine level was perceived as a "source of influence" but with less acceptance than the individual level (US: $M = 2.59$, $SD = .76$; Foreign: $M = 2.48$, $SD = .75$), whereas influence from the organizational level was perceived as "should have no influence" (US: $M = 1.13$, $SD = .34$; Foreign: $M = 1.34$, $SD = .46$).

Social Capital: Journalists' Interaction with Politicians

Correspondents perceived their own experiences as the dimension influencing their work the most. Hence, it was concluded that perceived autonomy exists when journalists' interactions matter. This data analysis showed that the idea of social capital (i.e., social interaction between reporters and sources as representing a capital or a resource for a reporter) can be conceptualized as influence from journalists' own experiences and interactions. In other words, journalists can most likely convert their networks into recognition if their own experiences and interactions matter for their reporting. The findings show that correspondents are more likely to perceive this kind of influence as important for their reporting than influences from the routine or

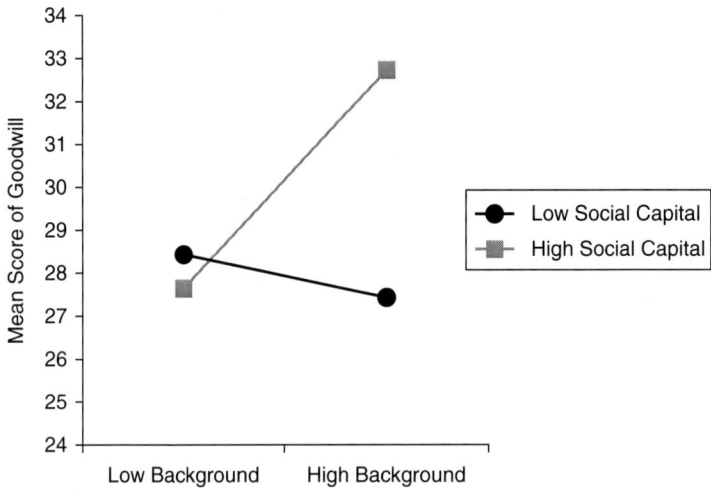

Figure 3.6 Correspondents' Perception of Goodwill, Based on Social Capital and Homophily.

organizational levels and that they are most likely accept their own experiences as an influence on their work, as it reflects their ideal of institutionalized cultural capital (i.e., how journalists should perform their jobs). The more correspondents' individual experiences matter for news stories, the more autonomy and power a journalist holds within the journalism field.

As shown in figure 3.6, correspondents' perceptions of sources' backgrounds significantly influence their perceptions of sources' goodwill if they have high social capital (i.e., if their own experiences are important for their news outputs). If news organizations prohibit correspondents from influencing their reporting, correspodents' perceptions are not predictive of their news outcomes. This might seem logical, but it puts into question the importance of a disseminator role and what it means to say that "journalists should be objective and detached."

Implications for Media Representations of Politicians

The goal of social science theories is not so much to explain things but to use explanations to predict phenomena (Shoemaker et al., 2004). In other words, explaining journalists' perceptions is the only meaningful way to understand journalism if applied as predicting news content. Hence, this section explicates media representations of politicians to integrate news reporting, or what Deuze (2005) theorized as representations of multiculturalism as dependent variables into a framework of journalism's multiculturalism gatekeeping.

Hall (1997) discussed representation as meanings given to images and stories depicted in the media. Compared to an older view of representation, where it was believed that representation is a reflection or distortion of reality, Hall (1997) argued that it is rather a presentation of a meaning that is already in society that is presented and depicted by the media. In line with field theory, a meaning that already exists in society relates to the idea of social space, which can be compared to a geographic space within which regions are divided (Bourdieu, 1989).

What is important in our understanding of social space is that the closer the journalists, politicians, and institutions are, the more properties of social, cultural, and economic capital they share. A sociology of social world perceptions (i.e., sharing similar values and norms) are perceptions from a particular position in a social space and are thus taken from a certain viewpoint. There is no doubt that journalists construct their visions of the world, but as Bourdieu (1989) argued, "structural constraints" color such perceptions: "The dispositions of agents, their habitus, that is, the mental structures through which they apprehend the social world, are essentially the product of the internalization of the structures of that world" (p. 18). Hence, media representations are expressions of social positions in which media organizations operate. The argument can be made that habitus structures not only perception and practices but also representations (i.e., the coverage of news sources).

Furthermore, the idea of social positions implies that a journalist's habitus is a sense of one's place but also "a sense of the place of others" (Bourdieu, 1989). Bourdieu (1998a) explained that journalists play a central role in the social world because, among the producers of public discourse, it is they who wield the most powerful means for circulating and imposing these. In other words, journalists occupy a privileged position in the symbolic struggle to bring attention to events, persons, and ideas, as well as set the news agenda. Also, Bourdieu pointed out that the strongest part of communication is its unconscious aspect, those things with which we communicate but about which we never communicate (such as economic and cultural capital). Bourdieu stated that journalism is "a very powerful profession made up of very fragile individuals" (p. 327).

Journalism scholars have acknowledged variations in newsroom practices: "The way a newsroom operates…influences how news is selected and shaped" (Shoemaker and Vos, 2009, p. 63). However, the variables behind those practices are the structural constraints that maintain and structure perceptions and practices. A news organization's position in a social field structures the practice of journalists working for this organization. For example, a journalist working for *The New York Times* or the *Washington Post* might have more access to sources because of the reputation of his or her company. Field theory contextualizes Gatekeeping Theory and enhances our understanding of why some sources make it through the "gate" and how.

Research shows that perceptions of source credibility are related to the quality aspect of news coverage (i.e., positive coverage), whereas it is not related to the amount of news coverage (Yoon, 2005). Shoemaker (1984) argued that more deviant groups are reported less favorably but not less prominently. Hence, in line with field theory, social positions structure meaning construction of news sources but do not structure the amount of news coverage.

The following findings from various research studies become more meaningful when considered under a social structure idea of field theory—that is, how journalists' habitus sense places and meanings. For example, Rothman and Lichter (1985) found that journalists who are overwhelmingly liberal in their opinion viewed liberals as more credible sources than conservatives. Starck and Soloski (1977) argued that closeness with a source affects the way journalists write their stories and their treatment of that source in stories. On the other hand, the constraints from organizational needs subordinate any personal ideology (Berkowitz, 1987). Peer-group pressure is another important factor that can influence reporters' source use (Donsbach, 2004; Grey, 1966). In such a case, it can be argued that through peer-group pressure, field position becomes more articulated and more naturalized as quasi-objectified and legitimized. Powers and Fico (1994) found that the three most influential variables on source usage were source credibility, source accessibility, and time pressure. In fact, 96 percent of respondents indicated that source credibility was often or always influential on source usage. Gans (1980) provided evidence that reporters act to protect the commercial and political interests of their media organization (i.e., to reinforce their position in the field). Powers and Fico (1994) argued that reporters at the most prestigious newspapers indicate they are able to resist internal and external pressures. This might be because they can profit from their cultural capital, which is congruent with the idea of journalistic capital. The more journalistic capital a news organization embodies, the more the news organization is resistant against external pressures (Hanitzsch, 2011). The more cultural capital a particular reporter within that news organization holds, the more his or her judgment matters for reporting.

In the final regression model (see table 3.5), goodwill and a similar background between the source and the reporter lead to a more positive coverage of the politician. As previous results showed, the professional contexts in which journalists operate hinder or allow journalists' perception to become story elements. In interpersonal communication contexts, the relationship between source credibility, believability, and likeability (Teven, 2008) is well-established; so is the relationship between perceived homophily and perceived attraction (L. L. McCroskey et al., 2006). As this current study shows, in a journalism context, professional constraints may hinder such interpersonal communication perceptions manifesting themselves in news stories. The findings resonate with normative assumptions of journalists as journalists provide a public service, are objective, impartial, neutral, and fair (Deuze, 2005). However, if journalists are impartial, neutral, and detached, where is the meaning coming from that they attach to stories? Professional obligations require journalists to switch to a more attached role as journalists' selection process implies leaving

Table 3.5   Predicting Source Valence in News Story by Perceived Homophily, Source Credibility, and Perceived Autonomy

	β	T
Demographics		
Gender	.029	0.563
Homophily		
Attitude	−.056	−0.600
Background	.172	2.005*
Source Credibility		
Competence	.123	1.288
Trustworthiness	−.065	−0.553
Goodwill	.265	2.478*
Social Capital	.200	2.390*
Routine Influence	−.092	−1.094
Organization Influence	.070	0.883

Note: $F(9,85) = 2.448$, $p < .001$; $R = .425$; $R^2 = .180$.
* Significant at the .05 level.
** Significant at the .001 level.

something out because something else is covered. In other words, the selection process requires journalists to attach meaning to some stories to have them considered, whereas less important information is kept out of the story.

Summary: Sourcing Tendencies in the 21st Century

The above findings on how correspondents define professional autonomy are contradictory to a Hierarchy of Influence model, which predicts that organizational and routine-level influences are stronger forces than individual-level influences (Shoemaker and Vos, 2009). On the contrary, from within the field, journalists perceive that their own experience (i.e., the individual level) should have the strongest influence on their news reports. By measuring news-gathering variables on an individual level and not relying solely on demographic variables (e.g., gender, years in the profession, political preferences), this study contributes to the understanding of how interactions with sources and social psychological factors such as source credibility and perceived homophily explain valence of news sources in media outputs. In light of a technological shift, the profession of journalism may shift from a profession of powerful gatekeepers influenced by organizational constraints to a profession of information exchange based on social relations (Bruns, 2005; Singer, 2010). This underlines the importance of studying interpersonal communication within a journalism context.

The results suggest that whether or not correspondents perceive politicians as sharing a similar background is predictive of how sources are eventually framed in news stories. In addition, this study shows that positions as explained by the perception of journalists are stronger forces of valence in news and in the tone of the source coverage if correspondents have more autonomy. Professional autonomy is conceptualized as institutionalized cultural capital (i.e., disseminator role) and as social capital (i.e., own experiences with sources influence the news outcome). In both cases, professional autonomy significantly predicts news outcomes by the social position that journalists hold in the journalism field. Hence, one can witness greater expressions of journalists' social positions and their perceptions in their representation of politicians if they are less influenced by pressures from their organizations that structure their work meaningfully. On the other hand, the news-gathering process must be conceptualized as an important indicator of how journalists' work is structured. If they have more autonomy, they are more likely to have direct access to politicians. And if they have more access, their construction of news sources is a way to preserve the field—that is, to reinforce the journalist's position in the field by referring not only to sources' field positions and ideas but also to a journalist's ideas and ideals because of the assumed similarity between the source and the journalist's own attitudes.

On the other hand, the results revealed that correspondents with less autonomy construct representations based on external forces or internal stronger forces stemming from the autonomous pole (i.e., from other media). If correspondents hold less autonomy, their positions are not predictive of how they frame politicians. Hence, the structuring force of accumulation of capital defines the constructive journalists' work output to a high extent. Journalists who have less autonomy are likely to be more fluid in their expression or more vulnerable to external influences or influences from the powerful end of the field. This is logical, as agents struggling for recognition may be more likely to adapt to the powerful institutionalized cultural capital in the field as they legitimize journalism as a profession. Furthermore, adherence to the established status system will eventually determine journalists' position in the hierarchy of the newsroom (Darnton, 1975).

Conceptualizating Sourcing in DC

Based on the web survey, five important findings can be summarized to conceptualize the source-reporter relationship in a transnational news environment.

(1) Attitude Similarity Positively Affects Perceptions of Source Credibility

The more journalists perceive themselves to be similar to a political source, the more they will perceive that source to be competent, trustworthy, and caring about the audience. Hence, the more in common correspondents and sources have in terms of attitudes and values, the higher the perception of the source's credibility.

(2) Personal Contact Matters for Perception

Once a journalist meets a political source in person, similarities of values influence the perception of the source's credibility. Without personal contact, such perceptions were much less important. Higher amount of social presence in personal interviews may contribute to a higher amount of autonomy because journalists are on the ground and hence their perceptions might be more likely to influence the stories they report because of their unique opportunity to access and thus their becoming a unique channel of information gathering.

(3) The Use of Social Media Decreases Trustworthiness and Goodwill

Correspondents might still perceive the personal interview and personal access as the most credible interaction with sources, and hence sourcing material from social media might be considered less credible than personal contact. This shows that social media does not replace personal contact as major credible source of information in DC.

(4) Role Conception Matters for Journalists' Perception of Sources

Perceived homophily will produce more positive perceptions of source credibility, only to the extent that journalists embrace the disseminator role. This was fully supported for the attitude homophily dimension but not for the background homophily dimension, however.

(5) Perception Affects Coverage

Perceived goodwill and background homophily leads to a more positive coverage of political sources.

The above five findings are further conceptualized on the cognitive and performative level as part of the transnational journalism culture model, bringing together those two levels to build a theoretical and analytical framework. The next step in understanding the source-reporter relationship in DC is to analyze those worldviews and occupational ideologies of journalists, which guide their professional performance—ideals less immediate to observation than their news content.

Note

1. A more detailed analysis of how measures on a normative level compare with the same questionnaire items on a more practical level (i.e., "last news story") can be found in Hellmueller (2012).

4

The Correspondents' Professional Worldviews of Their Interactions with Sources

You can have a cozy relationship with politicians, of course. You may become very cynical, or sometimes you may become sentimental. Or you develop friendship feelings for politicians.

—US correspondent, personal communication,
Washington, DC, January 2012

Correspondents are well aware that this job comes with the danger that they might become close to a political source. But what a journalist finds out from sources is not necessarily what they claim to be the truth. In essence, there is another element constituting journalism culture: the evaluative level of journalism culture, which provides the justification of social relations and a rationale for why the source is quoted in the news. At the evaluative level, journalists justify their news decisions based on their professional worldviews and epistemologies.

The previous empirical findings based on the cognitive and performative levels revealed that correspondents' perception of politicians sharing a similar background can influence how they frame sources in news stories. The results show that perceptions are more likely to influence the way sources are covered in news if correspondents have more autonomy. Professional autonomy is conceptualized as institutionalized cultural capital (i.e., disseminator role) and as social capital (i.e., one's own experiences with sources influencing the news outcome). In both cases, professional autonomy significantly predicts news outcomes by the social position that journalists hold in the journalism field.

In a way, this process leads to a homogenization of field positions and social positions of journalists and source expression in news. As well, correspondents on the autonomous side may set the agenda more than the ones on the heteronomous side. It is clear that these findings relate to social relations in the field and to how they affect news content. But—and this is a major limitation of field theory and the findings based solely on the survey—one does not want to reduce knowledge practices of journalists to be just a reflection of their social positions and their perception of similarity. Even though perceptions matter, they cannot explain everything. The field of journalism is a field of power in which social relations constitute one relation that is structuring knowledge practices. On the other hand, journalists' profession is based on its evaluative element—its truth telling most importantly (Kovach and Rosenstiel, 2001)—and thus, the justification of truth may well be reflected in how journalists respond to their social positions as news-structuring elements. Journalists justify their relationship with sources, for example, with whom they have to interact to provide a democratic function and inform the public about what is going on. If journalists have to "reveal as much as possible about (their) sources and methods" (Kovach and Rosenstiel, 2001, p. 92), then they have to participate in a social interaction with sources.

However, the information obtained must then be turned into news by justifying their truth claim. This is important because trust in news media depends on a professional and institutionalized form of presenting the truth. As watchdogs for the public, journalists are not supposed to report the news only based on their own relationships with sources, but audiences trust media because of their selectivity of facts, accuracy of depictions, and journalists' assessments (e.g., Kohring and Matthes, 2007), for which relationship with sources can provide a rich advantage but which are not the only criterion from which journalists abstract truth from knowledge. What a journalist knows from sources is not necessarily what they claim to be the truth. For example, the media provide an empirical justification with a sound bite or a quote to provide an epistemic relation from knowledge to truth, as evidenced in the *Los Angeles Times*: "Obama also used his speech to indirectly attack Romney's suggestion that veterans be offered vouchers to pay for private healthcare" (Memoli and Hennessey, 2012). In addition to their assessment, the *LA Times* quoted President Barack Obama: "I will not allow VA healthcare to be turned into a voucher system, subject to the whims of the insurance market," he said. "You don't need vouchers. You need the VA healthcare that you have earned and that you depend on" (Memoli and Hennessey, 2012).

Under the condition of social relations and epistemic relations (i.e., the truth-telling relation of what journalists know and how they objectify knowledge), it can be analyzed how knowledge claims establish themselves as powerful distinctions of truth or absence of truth in a field of power. In essence, that is what the qualitative in-depth study attempts to lay out. What is the epistemic justification (i.e., the evaluative level of journalism culture) of one position taker compared to other position takers on the other pole of the field? Based on the distinctions of the autonomous pole and the heteronomous pole, a different justification of truth may arise if there is a difference in how journalists express their relations with sources in their news stories. Specification of the qualitative part emerged from the web survey findings as an expansion of the findings from the first part of this research. That is the idea of mixed-method studies: "Initiation as the discovery of paradox and fresh perspectives may well emerge rather than constitute a planned intent" (Plano Clark and Creswell, 2008). Such an expansion may control for explanations apart from the original research study, a form of "soft control." Explanations based on mixing two or more paradigms can expand our knowledge of one research inquiry. Thus, the decisions for selecting a qualitative in-depth study were inductively based on the survey findings and were aimed to understand a journalism's multiculture from both social and epistemic positions.

Qualitative Interviews: Social Capital and Autonomy

At the end of the web survey, a final question asked correspondents if they were willing to participate in follow-up in-depth interviews. If they agreed to be part of the follow-up study, correspondents were asked to provide their contact details. A total of 33 correspondents showed their willingness to be interviewed. After the analysis of the quantitative data, those correspondents were divided into high, medium, and low in social capital. The distinction between the three groups—low (i.e., almost no influence of their own interaction with politicians), medium (i.e., some influence of their own interactions), and high social capital (i.e., strong influence of their interactions)—was based on the entire sample of the survey. Correspondents were divided into three equal groups of percentiles. The social capital scores for each correspondent included the normative score and the last news story score (range: 1–10) as a measure of their overall access to politicians. Hence, the first group (i.e., the low social capital group) was based on the range from 0 to 5.5 (33.33%), the second group (i.e., medium social capital) fell into the range between 5.56 and 7.50 (33.33%), and the group that scored the highest on social capital fell in the range between 7.51 and 10 (33.33%). The three categories of low, medium, and high social capital exist only in relation to each other; in fact, because some correspondents may have more access than others, the low social capital is conceptualized in comparison to the high social capital group. Correspondents who fall into the low social capital category have less access compared to correspondents in the high social capital group. Therefore, correspondents were divided into three categories according to the survey results. From the three groups, correspondents who were willing to be interviewed were grouped into the three ranges. From the 33 correspondents who were willing to participate in the follow-up interviews, 11 were found to score high on social capital, 15 were found in the medium social capital group, and 7 were in the low social capital group. All 33 correspondents were contacted in late November and early December 2011 to ask for their participation in a qualitative follow-up study. By December 15, 2011, a total of 12 correspondents agreed to participate. One correspondent was excluded from the analysis because he retired from his job and was occupied with book projects. However, his arguments were included in the analysis when appropriate, as he revealed interesting facts about interactions with politicians from a historical perspective with his 42 years of experience in DC. Table 4.1 provides an overview of all the correspondents who participated in the follow-up study.

Overview: Interview Process

The interviews were conducted in January 2012, in Washington, DC. Two interviews were conducted via Skype because the correspondents were not available for a personal meeting. The interviews ranged in length from 35 minutes to two hours, with an average length of 55 minutes. Interview questions allowed for flexibility and exploration. Some of the correspondents had a native language other than English. Furthermore, the interviewer's first language was not English. To avoid any confusion, some of the answers were repeated in the interviewer's own words to ensure that no information had been lost in translation. The purpose of these interviews was to understand how

Table 4.1 Participants of the Follow-Up Study

Medium	Years in DC	Net Native	Gender	Country of Reporting	Country of Origin
High Social Capital					
TV station	9 years or more	No	Male	US	Chile/US
TV station / Web-based media	5 years or more, but less than 9 years	No	Male	UAE	Lebanon
Newspaper, Radio, Magazine, Books	9 years or more	No	Male	US	US
Low Social Capital					
Newspaper	9 years or more	No	Male	US	US
News agency	More than 1 year, but less than 3 years	Yes	Male	Italy	Italy
Web-based media	3 years or more, but less than 5 years	Yes	Male	US	US
Newspaper, Radio station	9 years or more	No	Male	France, Morocco	France
Medium Social Capital					
TV station	5 years or more, but less than 9 years	No	Male	Switzerland	Switzerland
TV station	9 years or more	No	Female	Venezuela/ Colombia	Venezuela
TV station	More than 1 year, but less than 3 years	No	Male	Switzerland	Switzerland
Newspaper	More than 1 year, but less than 3 years	Yes	Male	Spain	Spain

cultural capital shapes social capital. There is relational ground for comparing the relative merits of knowledge claims in terms of their explanatory power (Maton and Moore, 2010). Knowledge is about something other than itself; it is a principle of ontological realism. Access to sources was long believed to be the foundation of building knowledge in a journalism field. Hence, social capital in the form of personal contact with sources seems to entail more epistemological and explanatory power than when gathering information based on the influence of routines or organizational constraints (e.g., quoting wire information).

The importance of access for journalism also reflects the close geographical positions to politicians in Washington, DC, such that US and foreign correspondents occupy: some of their offices are located at the National Press building, which is a block away from the White House and Congress and next to other news organizations. Hence, these correspondents enjoy more autonomy and may work closer with political sources and their colleagues in DC than with their news organizations back home or in another state (in the case of US correspondents).

Geographical and social proximity to journalists' sources reflect truth claims based on empirical justification (Hanitzsch, 2007a). The closer journalists are to their sources, the more likely they will be witnesses to an event and believe knowledge from their sources to be true. In other words, knowledge based on journalists' experiences is more powerful because the epistemic relation between knowledge and truth is based on empirical testing and justification. Hence, if information about an event is empirically tested (e.g., by meeting the source and having the source confirm that information), such information is likely to be turned into a truth claim. This entails more powerful epistemic claims than without empirical justification, and hence, the truth claim is expected to last longer than knowledge without empirical justification. Without confirmation of empirical justification, for example, knowledge based on other media can still be empirically tested and thus is negotiable as such knowledge. Once a truth claim is established, such a claim is more likely to be capable of generating epistemic profits (Maton, 2003).

The main limitation of field theory is that knowledge practices of journalists are reduced to a reflection of an agent's position in a field of power. In fact, Maton (2003) argued, "While acknowledging the will to power, one need not deny the will to truth. To do so would be to argue that every form of interest counts except for cognitive interest and that we research, teach, present, and read papers only in order to maximise capital" (p. 61). In essence, recognizing the role of nonsocial interests in producing journalism is crucial. Journalism does not involve only social power but also the power to tell the truth to produce a better knowledge of the world (i.e., epistemic power).

But what does the power to establish truth claims entail? What advantages can journalists gain from empirically justified truth claims? In the following interviews, the main concern was to investigate how journalists based on different social positions in the fields negotiate truth claims and articulate the evaluate level of journalism culture. Comparing correspondents with less access to correspondents with high access illuminates epistemic relations (the relationship between knowledge and a known truth) and how an epistemic relation relates to social relations (i.e., the closeness of sources and journalists based on social properties such as social class, economic background, status, etc.) or transcends social positions.

The quantitative analysis revealed background homophily to structure valence of sources in journalists' output. However, the expression of positive valence may not be based only on the background homophily variable, for example. Background homophily indicates closeness to a source, but it may well be that because reporters and sources share similar properties of a field, their ideas legitimize themselves in their objectification, what Donsbach (2004) labeled as quasi-objectification because of a shared understanding of truth. Hence, closeness may indeed follow a powerful epistemic claim of empirical justification of truth. Correspondents may socialize more with sources from their own countries because they speak the same language or share a similar taste, so their epistemic relations of truth are based on an empirical verification of truth claims, which may be more powerful in cases where empirical verification is embedded in the cultural capital of journalists. Knowledge from close sources is more likely to be turned into truth. Without doubt, the strongest effect of this is the case for TV journalists whose stories depend on personal contacts.

The following analysis applies a grounded theory approach in the sense that it demonstrates relations between cultural capital and social capital—between conceptual categories—and specifies the conditions under which such a relationship changes, emerges, or is maintained. In looking at the evaluative component of journalism culture, explanatory categories are investigated to foster the descriptive and predictive results from the quantitative analysis. On the other hand, the underlying belief of the research is that a scientific analysis is always an analysis based on a scientific position. Hence, while a constructivist idea of grounded theory understands everything to emerge from the data, this research follows a more structuralism-constructivist approach. In other words, every field inquiry is driven by theory as an expression of the researchers' position in the academic field. The constructivist part of such a paradigm provides the possibility that some themes (not yet identified before the data-collection process) may still emerge from the data.

Interview Questions

The interview questions were grouped according to a grounded theory logic, ranging from initial open-ended questions (e.g., "Tell me about your background: What motivated you to work as a political correspondent in the DC area?"), intermediate questions ("How does a political source monitor your reporting?"), to ending questions (e.g., "What does journalistic freedom mean to you?").

In-depth interviews force correspondents to elicit an interpretation of their daily news-gathering experiences—as Charmaz (2006) explained, "Intensive interviewing permits an in-depth exploration of a particular topic or experience and, thus, is a useful method for interpretive inquiry" (p. 25). Such interpretations are not necessarily and consciously activated in their practice. Correspondents' stories are narratives based on their points of view that serve specific purposes at a particular moment in time.

Overview: Analysis of Interviews

The interviews were analyzed in four phases. First, each interview was recorded and transcribed. In the end, about 100 pages' worth of interview data were produced, which provided the data material for the qualitative coding and the textual analysis that are now outlined.

Textual Analysis and Qualitative Coding

The process of coding the qualitative data in this research was based on Charmaz's (2006) practical guide through qualitative analysis, which structured the coding process as a whole: "Coding is the first step in moving beyond concrete statements in the data to making analytic interpretations" (p. 43). In the initial coding, decisions involved what to include in the analysis and what to leave out. Using the "constant comparison method" with the literature reinforced theoretical claims and theoretical statements, which build the selection criteria of where to focus while interpreting the textual statements. The coding process attempted to build a framework for an analysis, which was based on analytic frames provided by cultural and social capital literature (Charmaz, 2006; Glaser and Strauss, 1967). Based on the first coding process, an understanding of the data content emerged.

Initial Coding

The first step in research was to define the core conceptual categories. With the theoretical sampling and the comparisons of the three different groups of correspondents with each other, similarities and differences emerged that built up the conceptual categories of interest for this study. Hence, correspondents' understanding of cultural capital in its three forms (i.e., embodied, objectified, and institutionalized) was analyzed and compared as an expression of their position in the journalism field. That is, their answers were compared according to their social capital and perceived autonomy (i.e., whether or not their interactions influenced news content).

All answers were grouped into overall research questions according to correspondents' amount of social capital. Then they were coded in relation to their theoretical categories. A constant comparison method helped to redefine categories emerging from the data according to theoretical concepts from the literature. The comparison process allowed for new ideas and clues to emerge that had not been identified before the actual coding phase. Analytical distinctions were then drawn to account for different field positions and their explanations. Such distinctions further served validity claims in quantitative research, as it allowed the testing of theories in different contexts and enabled discussion of the construct validity of conceptual categories (e.g., under what condition does this phenomena occur?). Table 4.2 shows how a constant comparison method was put into practice. The embodied cultural capital stratified the answer of the three groups. The responses were set in contrast to each other to reveal differences and similarities between positions in the field; this is why the medium social capital is on the left side and not in the middle.

Statements from the correspondents were compared, and their keywords were coded for the sake of comparisons. The collected list with the keywords provided an understanding of each analytical category, its content, and its coding. At an early stage of the textual analysis, the enduring influence of embodied cultural capital was identified as shaping the objectified and institutionalized cultural capital. The transformation from embodied cultural capital (i.e., experiences, education) into objectified and institutionalized capital deserves further attention. If journalists learn from their own experiences or at universities that access is important to be recognized and to eventually become a Washington correspondent, such embodied cultural capital routines become strong forces to articulate their profession (e.g., sources make time for us; it is a very powerful job) but also to justify why they were hired as a Washington correspondent. The privilege of being a DC correspondent is attributed to embodied cultural capital (e.g., a degree in international politics helping the correspondent understand the political processes in Washington).

Table 4.2   Constant Comparison Method

	High Social Capital	Low Social Capital	Medium Social Capital
Embodied Cultural Capital	"I was born in Chile. My father is a professor and my mother a dentist. I studied English and German. Then I came to the US to study journalism in Iowa. I became the managing editor of a college newspaper. After that, I worked for ESPN, which gave me a lot of access. People realized the reach of our organization; sources made time for us. It is a very powerful job."	"I have a degree in political science and a master's degree in journalism from the time when I studied in Milano, Italy. After graduation, I worked at the Italian Congress. I was embedded. I covered the Prime Minister Berlusconi. He is incredible. But the job was really exhausting. Coming to the US is great—it is the place of the new languages of politics."	"As a graduate in history and political science, I had always been interested in politics and international relations. When, after years of work as a political journalist and special correspondent, I was offered the post of US correspondent, it was of course a great opportunity I had to grab. To a journalist passionate by international politics, the post of U.S. correspondent is a great achievement. It is a privilege to work as such at a young age when for many journalists the DC post is often the last one before retirement."

Phase 2 included looking for keywords. When asking what defines journalism, keywords that appeared in every interview were truth, objectivity, and professionalism. Hence, correspondents are well aware that their profession is based on specific tasks related to truth. And this relationship defines the field of journalism from a global logic. Objectivity still serves as the gold standard of news gathering. The articulation of it may well be a justification for journalists' adherence to a form of believed institutionalized cultural capital. In addition, objectivity is a defense strategy used to define the boundaries between journalism and new entrants to the field (e.g., the CNN iReporters). Objectivity as a definition of the journalism field may also serve as a weapon to prevent new entrants from getting established in the journalism field. Journalists reinforce the structural principle of the field, not exclusively via a defense strategy imposed by Western journalists but through a global strategy—for correspondents reporting for countries as diverse as Saudi Arabia, Morocco, Venezuela, and Colombia.

Focused Coding

After conceptual categories were established in close relationship with theoretical claims, research questions were answered by synthesizing and explaining the relationship between the cultural capital and the social capital and outlining this relationship based on field positions (i.e., across the three different groups of correspondents). Codes and data were constantly compared to each theoretical claim, and conceptual categories were redefined according to emerging ideas.

Axial Coding

One of the final coding stages is axial coding (Charmaz, 2006). In this process, adding subcategories to the major categories specifies dimensions of categories. This process creates a coherent understanding of the concept under investigation. Subcategories can be helpful in explaining how concepts relate to each other and can describe the concept more fully by answering questions such as when, where, why, who, and how. At the center of attention here are interactions, consequences, and conditions of the categories, which serve to explain concepts or constructs. In this stage, a deeper understanding of social and cultural capital was gained by putting the categories in context, adding more contexts to each answer, and explaining the reason for answers in more depth.

Theoretical Coding

Theoretical coding can move the results toward a theoretical end. In doing so, theoretical coding provides an understanding of where new findings may enhance existing theories and provides new knowledge about the relationships between concepts. Glaser (1978) defined theoretical coding as "how the substantive codes may relate to each other as hypotheses to be integrated into a theory" (p. 72). Thus, theoretical codes specify relationships among categories that were identified in the first phases of coding (Charmaz, 2006). Table 4.3 provides a summary of the entire coding process, from initial coding to theoretical coding.

As outlined in table 4.3, epistemic reflection as included in phase 3 is an important procedure before proceeding with the textual analysis. Wrestling with preconceptions is a worrisome concern in grounded theory work because every researcher brings with him or her a certain amount of an accumulated history, a set of ideas. Taken-for-granted assumptions may unconsciously influence coding decisions and become most evident if they are challenged and when they articulate themselves in a dissonant way. Deeply rooted assumptions decrease the likelihood of flexibility in the analysis. Most assumptions are not unsupported, however. One assumption challenged in this research, and which was at least hypothetically supported by previous studies (Willnat and Weaver, 2003), was the idea that access is the most important indicator of autonomy. If a journalist is skilled in the job and is accepted by sources, then he or she will be granted access as a sign of recognition. This assumption was supported by the quantitative survey of this research. In addition, for some of the foreign correspondents interviewed for the qualitative study, lack of access is incredibly frustrating:

> If you try to get an interview with a source at the Congress, they never have time for us. It is sometimes very, very hard to get firsthand information, and that is very, very frustrating. We read their opinions in other media, and that is frustrating again. (Foreign TV correspondent, personal communication, Washington, DC, January 2012)

According to the correspondent quoted above, access is granted to their TV station only one time out of seven. However, through the analysis of the qualitative interviews, a more nuanced interpretation of access could be gained in relation to the justification of truth. There are two conceptually different ways of approaching the truth. The first assumption about access—that access stands for autonomy—could not adequately interpret this segment of data without consulting new literature on the meaning behind "access" for journalists from different cultures. It is not only a question of class, gender, age, or whether or not journalists have high access to politicians. Justification of truth can be a driving force in whether journalists see access as enhancing or decreasing truth-telling strategies.

As discussed earlier in the literature review, Hanitzsch (2007a) pointed to this double meaning of access explicitly. In some countries, factual knowledge of observations, measurements, evidence, and experience constitute truth-telling obligations, whereas in other countries, an analytical knowledge is guiding a justification and an instrument for journalism's obligation to the truth. An analytical knowledge is acquired through an analytical justification of truth that accentuates reasoning, ideas, values, opinion, and analysis. Such different ideas of justification of access (whether access is a means to the truth or a force against the truth) can be explained by the concept of *illusio* that provides an understanding because of the sociological framework of field theory on which this study is based.

Table 4.3 Four Phases of Grounded Theory Analysis

Phase	Description of Analysis	Technique	Goals	Practical Achievements
Phase 1	– Transcribing interviews. – Note-taking. – Starting initial analysis. – Identifying indigenous categories.	Open coding—Look for word repetition.	– Capturing first impressions. – Modifying questions based on interviews (Respondents were pre-selected to ensure variety of correspondents—theoretical saturation).	– Creating a document for each correspondent. – Including a detailed summary after each transcript (including descriptions about respondents, field notes, capturing lifestyle themes emerging from interview location, and interactions with correspondents).
Phase 2	– Detailed reading and analysis of interviews. – Looking for emerging themes within theoretical and empirical framework of cultural and social capital (embedded grounded theory analysis)—*habitus embedded in grounded theory.* – Understanding epistemic reflexivity: analysis from a position guides emerging themes of grounded theory *Structuralism–Constructivist.*	– Open coding. – Applying cultural capital concept (embodied, objectified, and institutionalized state)—open coding *keywords in context.* – Looking for emerging themes (conversion rate) guided by scientific habitus (i.e., the importance of conversion rates within the discussion of capital).	– Looking for keywords. – Taking decisions to include or exclude themes. – Understanding the framework of cultural and social capital.	– Initial coding of the table. – Taking decisions to include themes. – Pre-coding on paper/comments on each transcript. – Writing down future steps for coding. – Clarifying statements that need more elaboration to be fully coded. – Clarifying misunderstandings or grammatically misleading statements.

Continued

Table 4.3 Continued

Phase	Description of Analysis	Technique	Goals	Practical Achievements
Phase 3	– Reading the transcripts again, dividing questions into research question categories. – Understanding differences/similarities. – Developing mindfulness for emerging themes among RQs. – Epistemic reflexivity.	**Constant Comparison Method** Open coding – Axial coding relating categories and concepts to each other (deductive and inductive thinking). – Comparison coding, looking for differences and similarities.	– Adding/revising coding. – Finding similarities / differences. looking for emerging themes, not necessarily related to scientific habitus.	– Creating new documents from answers from correspondents but organizing answers according to theoretical sampling and research questions. – Creating 1–4 file(s) for each research question combined with correspondents' answers.
Phase 4	Looking for connectors/transitions between social and cultural capital.	*Linguistic analysis* Looking for words and phrases that indicate relationship (examples below). Causal relationships: because, since, and as a result. Conditional relationship: if, then, rather, than, and instead of. Time-oriented relationships: before, after, then, and next.	Finding connectors between social and cultural capital. – Searching for missing information. Transitions: how do correspondents transition from cultural capital or social capital to another topic.	Creating new documents with connectors. Perusing through texts and marking them up with different colors.

Bourdieu's (1979) concept of *illusio* means that the structure of a social field can be meaningful for a particular group only. It should not refer to the fact that agents are deluded. The word *illusio* was chosen to account for the idea that there is no authentic reality to contrast with the present, except perhaps a world that has learned to live with its own arbitrariness (Crossley, 2005). Professional ideas of journalism exist in relation to social fields. Different meanings developed in societies according to cultural historical reasons. Those meanings are strong forces shaping perception because they legitimize journalism as a profession for a particular social system and for the audience they eventually report to in their work. In a transnational journalism context, this concept of audience can be more fluid, but it remains a force whereby journalists gain recognition from readers, viewers, and followers.

However, taken-for-granted assumptions may shape a majority of cross-cultural journalism research that focuses on developed and developing countries, as they generally reinforce normative ideals in a rank order where Western values are believed to be more professional (Josephi, 2005). Therefore, the following paragraphs provides a multicultural framework for the theoretical coding to rethink taken-for-granted assumptions.

Multicultural Framework of Analysis

From these discussions, it seems clear that a framework that works properly across cultures is needed for the analysis. Conceptual stability and validity in diverse cultural contexts are almost never achieved. Hanitzsch's (2007a) piece on journalism culture is an exception. He pointed out a reference of universal concepts that are used in different cultures but to different degrees. In other words, such global concepts are of great theoretical importance to understanding journalism cultures across national borders. They are important because they highlight similarities and differences based on the same concept and thus offer benefits of comparison because culture is explained in relation to other cultures. By comparing universal concepts, cultural logics can manifest themselves in comparisons. Such differences would remain invisible if they had not been applied to a global context because there would be no variation of these concepts. Such global concepts, then, help to tap the cultural diversity of journalism in a transnational context.

Therefore, in phase 3, the constant comparison method allowed comparisons of how journalists evaluate such global concepts and whether such evaluations can be explained by their performative ele-ment of journalism culture (i.e., their access to sources in their last news story) in the way journalists do their work (Hanitzsch, 2007a).

Practices are supposed to be shaped by evaluative elements—that is, such evaluative elements are supposed to shape professional per-formance through these deep structures, mostly unconsciously. To enhance the validity of the findings, the interpretation of the cultural capital in conversion with the idea of social capital of journalists was based on research about journalism cultures around the world. For example, universal traits in journalism have been conceptualized by Deuze (2005) as ideal-type elements. According to Deuze (2005), journalists provide a public service; are objective, impartial, and neu-tral; have a sense of immediacy; desire to be autonomous; and have a sense of ethics, validity, and legitimacy. Multiculturalism and mul-timedia are changing and challenging such ideal types of a cultural and technological development in the field of journalism (Deuze, 2005). For the interviewed Washington correspondents, objectivity, fairness, and independence remained cornerstones of their journalism ideology. However, if journalists' first obligation is to the truth, then justification of belief becomes the driving force of journalism and its ideal types (its evaluative level of journalism culture). Hence, if cor-respondents refer to objectivity, it is important to underline claims of knowledge and truth (i.e., how objectivity is embedded in practice) to understand how correspondents interact with sources. If truth is the evidence of knowledge for journalism, then justification of truth is the driving force for understanding interactions with sources, which pro-vide potential truth. In other words, journalists who strive to have as much access as possible to sources must have a different understand-ing of how truth can be justified or achieved through their interactions with sources than those who prefer to sit in their offices or at home to keep a professional distance from their sources. With an emergence of new technologies and multimedia platforms, such truth claims may be transformed or adapted to the new multimedia environment. Furthermore, in a multicultural environment, justifications based on cultures become evident in their comparison.

The next paragraph summarizes the findings from the four phases of coding. Within that process, clustering provided prewriting tech-niques for starting the analysis. It produced a chart of work and laid out a diagram of relationships. Different forms of clusters were applied to see how concepts fit together differently. For example, one cluster was put together by a comparison method between field positions. In another cluster, experiences of embodied, objectified, and institution-alized cultural capital built up a different narrative of how clusters helped to see axial codes. In such a form, connections and conver-sion rates between the three different states of cultural capital could be identified, whereas in the first cluster, differences and similarities between field positions might reveal heterogeneous understandings of cultural and social capital. The clustering process emerged into a stage of chaos first, from where it created a way of moving through the material more analytically. In essence, the content and findings of the categories as outlined below explicate the dimensions of the catego-ries. In addition, looking for connectors (e.g., words indicating causal, conditional, or time-oriented relationships) refined compositions of social and cultural capital and conversions of such.

The Findings of the Evaluative Level

The findings of the interviews are structured according to a Gatekeeping Theory logic (Shoemaker and Vos, 2009) and explain how levels of gatekeeping structure position in the journalism field. The first set of findings explains how the journalism field is structured by powerful forces of the political field (i.e., extra-media level or social institutional level forces). Levels of gatekeeping are reconceptualized as forces that structure journalists' positions from where their social percep-tions construct frames of politicians. Forces are not set in a hierar-chy but rather are defined by their structuring power. For example, if the political field imposes more power over how journalists select information than media organizations impose over journalists, then such social institutional level influences are stronger forces that define positions of correspondents. Positions are important to understand because they structure correspondents' viewpoints. If correspondents have more autonomy from the political field, they are more likely to impose their evaluative components on their practice because the political field structures their viewpoints less. Or to put in another way, the correspondents are more likely to convert their cultural capi-tal into practice.

Finding 1: Structural Forces of the Political Field

It would be naïve to believe that journalists are not exposed to struc-turing forces other than their own ideals of normative standards and relationships with sources. Hence, their sense-making processes are highly structured by forces that are structuring their positions through rules and frameworks that politicians set in a struggle to take control over media messages. Two main structuring principles stemming from the political field emerged from the data: first, foreign correspondents still struggle in getting access to important policy makers—for example, they have to show their passports when they attend a press briefing at the White House if they are not US citizens. One foreign correspondent explained:

> They simply don't care about foreign media, because they don't bring them any votes, and U.S. politicians are on a permanent campaign. As an example, even when we had to cover the controversy surrounding UBS, the senator in charge of the Congress hearings never accorded us an interview, simply because his agenda is already charged, and giving an interview to a Swiss journalist is definitely not a priority. (Personal communication, Washington, DC, January 2012)

In addition to US politicians' awareness of tailoring messages to a US audience, the political field may lay out strict rules on how to interact with and quote official sources. For example, the State Department and the Obama administration have ground rules for interviewing officials. As one foreign correspondent stated, "America under this president [President Obama] is very tightly controlled; they will only tell you what they want to tell you. It is very orchestrated" (foreign correspondent, personal communication, Washington, DC, January 2012). Following the rules is the ticket to the White House, for example. Correspondents follow the rules because they are granted access in exchange. "If you break the ground rules, you will no longer go the White House, period. This is frustrating because you are reporting what is happening, you are part of the rules, you follow them blindly" (foreign correspondent, personal communication, Washington, DC, January 2012).

Table 4.4 lists the ground rules for interviewing State Department officials. These rules must be agreed upon at the beginning of any conversation. The officials determine most of the ground rules, which reflects the political field's structuring power of the autonomy of correspondents. By decreasing correspondents' power, politicians increase their power of delivering knowledge to an audience.

The US State Department represents one of the most important sources for foreign correspondents due to its nature of dealing with

Table 4.4   Rules for Interviewing State Department Officials (as of May 2012)

On the Record	Information may be quoted directly and attributed to the official by name and title.
On Background	The official's remarks may be quoted directly or paraphrased and are attributed to a "State Department official" or "Administration official," as determined by the official.
On Deep Background	The source cannot be quoted or identified in any manner, not even as "an unnamed source." The information is usually couched in such phrases as "it is understood that" or "it has been learned." The information may be used to help present the story or to gain a better understanding of the subject, but the knowledge is that of the reporter, not the source. No information provided may be used in the story. The information is only for the reporter's background knowledge.
Off the Record	Nothing of what the journalist is told may be used in the story. The information is meant only for a reporter's knowledge.

Source: US Department of State, 2012.

foreign issues. The following is a quote from a foreign correspondent explaining the structuring setting of news gathering at the White House compared to the State Department:

If you go to the White House briefing, in the front row, AP will always get the first question. Then you have the correspondents of the major networks and media organizations, ABC, CBS, NBC, Fox, CNN, and Reuters. Those people are gathering for an American audience with 300 million people in this country. At the White House, if you are giving a briefing, you are not giving a briefing to someone in Saudi Arabia, you are addressing the American audience. Then, Jay Carney [Obama's spokesperson], when he answers a question by CNN, he knows that he is answering for the American audience, and CNN is influential, because it is reaching them. Now, if I want to ask a question, he may give me the chance to ask the question. But I'm not important. They [the briefings] are usually geared at the White House for an American audience. Now, if you go to the State Department, it's totally different. Most people of the State Department are foreigners; more than 75% sitting in the briefing rooms are foreigners. They will give you an equal chance because we are gathering for a foreign audience. (Personal communication, Washington, DC, January 2012)

Other informative sources that foreign correspondents rely on are people working at universities, think tanks, and colleagues working for foreign media who speak the same language or are from a culturally similar background. Furthermore, foreign correspondents remain tied to their home cultures and languages primarily because they report for such an audience. In addition, language and cultural similarities among foreign correspondents play an important role in how they share information and socialize:

> In the US, American journalists are very, very competitive against each other. For example, when you are covering something with other journalists, you will see the attitude: "This is for me; I won't share that, etc." If they [correspondents] are not working for the same media or the same country, they don't care. Latin American journalists are more willing to share information with me. They are more willing to share information than Americans—because we come from countries where we are more willing to help and share information. (Foreign TV correspondent, personal communication, Washington, DC, January 2012)

Finding 2: Institutionalized Cultural Capital

The political field in Washington, DC structures the work of correspondents in such a transnational environment. Hence, the environment where journalists work and interact with sources seems to determine their positions in the field to a higher extent than the political systems in their home countries. Looking at how journalism is practiced, such system factors (social system–level influences as pointed out in Gatekeeping Theory) in a transnational working environment may become less important because of the immediacy between correspondents abroad and their sources—the starting point from where information is transformed into news. However, it is exactly this immediacy that is articulated as problematic when dealing with politicians:

> How can we be in the middle and not taking sides with anyone? That is the difficult part of our profession. (Foreign TV correspondent, personal communication, Washington, DC, January 2012)

Being in the middle and being balanced and impartial remains a persistent myth of journalistic behavior in Washington, DC. All journalists who participated in this study acknowledged the importance of journalistic objectivity and balance. But as this study shows, how the myth plays out in practice may vary according to journalists' institutionalized cultural and social capital (i.e., their position in the field and their closeness to the political field).

Correspondents' positions in terms of how much access they have to political sources revealed sense-making paradoxes, which underline the difficulties to understand behavior and unexplained variance of the quantitative analysis. For example, correspondents with a high amount of social capital may well be aware that their reporting is influenced by politicians, but they nevertheless accept this influence in exchange for access.

Furthermore, with close social proximity, journalists are more likely to establish an understanding of politicians' backgrounds, with that understanding being based on their own positions and driven by a habitus of comparing one's position to others.

On the surface, the correspondents seem to agree to normative standards such as objectivity, fairness, balance, and impartiality, but how normative ideals are applied in practice varies in how journalists cope with their dependence on sources (i.e., how balance plays out in dealing with sources). For example, relationships with sources can be defined by journalism's normative ideal of accuracy. One US correspondent defined his own rule of accuracy in the following way: "The degree to which a reportage is fair and objective is in direct relation to your proximity to the person about whom you are writing." This rule was defined after an experience with a source who was "not only the city engineer; he also attended the same church as my parents and was a frequent visitor to our home." An embodied cultural capital (i.e., experience with a source) and components of social relations, such as homophily, converts the cultural capital of accuracy into an institutionalized form of cultural capital. Early career experiences build the bases for the transformation of embodied cultural capital into objectified and institutionalized cultural capital (i.e., into how journalism ought to be).

Embodied cultural capital (i.e., experiences and education) is formative of institutionalized cultural capital. This also holds true for an earlier example of with whom to share information. Foreign correspondents in that example had learned to share information as a way to improve their stories and hence have institutionalized the task of information sharing with colleagues. However, in the United States, they remain resistant to a competitive media environment and continue sharing information with their colleagues who share the same language and culture. Hence, the conversion of embodied cultural capital into institutionalized capital is a formative phase, which is vulnerable to external influence; but once established, institutionalized cultural capital remains resistant to change.

This could not only be observed in the mentioned examples. In the high social capital category, journalists had learned early through their experiences with sources that access is an important success factor in journalism: "The great benefit is access; when you are quoting second-hand information, you do not have the credibility—because the viewer is trusting someone on the ground more than someone who is not there." The issue is with the viewer as part of the institutionalized form of cultural capital. Access legitimizes itself through the acceptance of this kind of journalists' assessment (e.g., being close to your sources) among the audience. The conversion principle between the audience and the journalist in the example is based on mutual trust and trust mechanisms. Again, trust reduces uncertainty if access is believed to be the justification of truth for the correspondent's audience and sources. It does so by establishing an understanding of what has to be "paid" (i.e., the time and effort required to gain access) or exchanged to be right and true.

Normative ideals of journalism manifest themselves in their justification of relationships with sources. If accuracy is believed to be achieved through a close relationship then closeness to a source is a resource of social capital (i.e., a social relationship and membership in a social network that is required to perform a normative ideal of journalism).

Now, how do correspondents come to establish a system of a trust mechanism on which they unconsciously rely on a taken-for-granted logic? Early practical or educational experiences are important forces (i.e., embodied cultural capital) that are transformed into objectified cultural capital (i.e., expressed in journalists' everyday news gathering) and manifested through routines into legitimized forms of institutionalized cultural capital, such as the following quote: "My professor at Columbia taught me that we are all born with some biases, depending on what our backgrounds are and who our parents are and what they do." This statement came from a US web correspondent with low social capital. Low social capital was institutionalized cultural capital for this correspondent because "to understand what these inherent biases are, I have to step back and understand what my point of view might be and then do some reporting that is alternative of what my instinct might be or what your parents or sources think."

In other words, the qualitative analysis shows that positions on the heteronomous pole—where the conceptualization of the heteronomous pole is based on a Western ideal of high access representing the autonomous pole—do not necessarily reflect a dependence on external field logics. Such a position also can be an expression of an institutionalized form of journalism to prevent journalists from reporting their own biases. Furthermore, US correspondents are not necessarily drawn to the autonomous pole. It depends on their institutionalized cultural capital.

To summarize, correspondents with low or high social capital both share the structuring force of the embodied cultural capital, which defines their institutionalized cultural capital. To elaborate on that, an established form of institutionalized cultural capital is based on embodied capital such as what US and foreign correspondents had learned at universities or from early experiences in the profession in the form of objectified cultural capital. This was recognized as valuable because access is crucial to building credibility among audiences. However, against a previous assumption of the quantitative survey, access does not in any case define social capital. To conclude, positions in the journalism field are most fundamentally determined by their embodied cultural capital and institutionalized cultural capital, which refine correspondents' social capital and their strategies of engaging with politicians.

In the next section, such strategies of social relations unique to the journalistic profession are outlined in context of their epistemic relation: a journalist's institutionalized cultural capital, which is their justification of truth. An understanding is developed by clustering findings according to their position in the field. Hence, journalists with high social capital are discussed first, followed by a comparison with correspondents with low social capital to account for different approaches to justifications of truth within the field.

Finding 3: Truth Claims and Social Capital Practices as Language of Legitimization

High Social Capital

Correspondents with a high amount of access to sources share the presumptions or the tendency of an absolute sense of objectivity ("true objectivity is important"), a perception of reality that guides their interactions with sources. Foremost, a strong professional distance between sources and reporters is not necessary, as truth ought to be in the sources and not created. Hence, the empirical justification of truth provides the basis for such a social relationship because experience and empirical evidence are tools for establishing a truth claim. There exists a relationship between "what is said" and "what exists" (Hanitzsch et al., 2011). On the other hand, journalists who are "not on the ground," as one TV correspondent from Lebanon mentioned, "are not doing a proper job." For this correspondent, a proper job based on the cultural capital of truth justification can be converted into trust and symbolic capital on the side of the audience: "audiences prefer eyewitnesses" (foreign correspondent with high social capital, personal communication, Washington, DC, January 2012).

Hanitzsch et al. (2011) compared how different countries approach truth on the objectivism dimension. However, their findings for country scores did not reveal any consistent pattern for both objectivism and empiricism when comparing different countries. By bringing social capital into the analysis, it seems plausible that the medium itself might be the stronger force of objectivism as a form of reality perception than the country as a unit of analysis. For example, for TV journalists—as is the case for most of the interviewed journalists in the high social capital category—TV as a medium depends on eyewitness material because it is different from print in that the accounts are based on eyewitness facts:

> My number one goal is very simple: it is to get a sound bite. You know, you could tell the story yourself. [...] And there is this distance you should keep, of course, we use them and they use us. They want to get their message across and we need sound bites. (US TV correspondent, high social capital, personal communication, January 2012)

In other words, if the audience is used to trusting the pictures and sound bites on the TV screen, then the sound bites are a strong force to establish a conversion rate of how trust on the audience side can be established in exchange for the performance of professional skills. In such a case, then, providing an understanding of who has the better position is secondary, as audience members can draw their own interpretations. Because of the established rules of verifying a story, the closeness to political sources is based on the aim of verifying information: "You establish trust if you reveal exclusive information—two sources who were established within an executive office—that is the simple secret" (foreign correspondent, personal communication, Washington, DC, January 2012). The correspondent gave an example:

> I wrote a story that Vice President Biden will go to Iraq to finalize the deal with the Iraqis. And I said that he would go there the first week

of December [2011] and troops will be out ahead of schedule. For two weeks, I was very nervous because of the story I wrote. But it indeed happened. And all troops left before Christmas. Whoever received my story remembered that I predicted that. "Oh my god, XX told us about this a month before." This is how you establish trust. I just knew from my sources. But it was not only one source. (Personal communication, Washington, DC, January 2012)

Because truth measurements rely on eyewitnessing, a close relationship with a source benefits such an epistemological logic. As one correspondent detailed, a well-established newsroom "will not publish any piece of information without making sure through the filters that it is trustworthy." This is extremely important because "You make one mistake and you ruin everything. Any mistake that is made by you or your company ruins your relationship with your sources." Hence, a falsification method as empirical justification of truth is established, and correspondents are aware that sources are their most critical judges: as one foreign correspondent of high social capital said, "if you are faithful to the source, then you are good and you can maintain a trusted relationship with the source" (personal communication, Washington, DC, January 2012). Table 4.5 contrasts the relationship between epistemic and social relations. Social relations with politicians are established as empirical justifications of truth. Because correspondents believe that objectivity is a goal they strive for, they empirically test their sources (i.e., gain as much access as possible) to verify knowledge and establish truth claims established through methods of eyewitnessing and the principle of falsification. A distinction is drawn between journalists who are doing a proper job (are "on the ground") and journalists who are not doing a proper job ("who are not on the ground and who have no access").

Low Social Capital

For correspondents with low social capital, closeness to a source is not the only means to the truth: "You can be friendly with sources but not friends" (US correspondent, low social capital, personal communication, Washington, DC, January 2012). Most of the respondents in this group did not believe objectivity exists. Furthermore, they believed that keeping a professional distance from sources is crucial so that trust can be established among their audiences. However, even if a social relationship with sources is based on a rather subjective or multi-perspectival analysis, the epistemic relation is still key to

Table 4.5   High Social Capital: Epistemic and Social Relations

Epistemic Relation (Empirical Justification of Truth)	Social Relation
"Evidence and experience are the basis of truth."	"You believe every shit they are telling you and you report it."
"Truth must be pursued."	"Experiences with sources help me."
"True objectivity is important."	"Someone who is not on the ground is not doing a proper job—audiences prefer eyewitnesses."
"You and your stories become part of the rules. We are reporting what is happening; we cannot break the rules."	
"Checking that it is done in a professional way is the most important part of a newsroom to verify truth."	Your loyalty is for your company, not for the politician.
"If people trust you, then you are doing a good job."	"They are using us as a medium, not me as a person."
	"You can be at a party with anyone, you can go golfing with anyone, you can marry their daughter; I don't care as long as they don't want you to work for them."

Note: All statements in quotation marks are culled from the qualitative interviews involving correspondents with high access to politicians.

understanding how truth is established based on knowledge. Personal contact may be beneficial, but it is not the foundation of the epistemic relation; it does not reflect the epistemic relation to objectify knowledge into truth. One of the correspondents, for example, mentioned time as a crucial element to a move toward truth: "I like spending a lot of time on a story; I enjoy it; it is my pride." Organizational guidelines are less important in understanding facts and self-reflection is more important. The underlying idea is that an understanding of field positions can illuminate how social capital can be conceptualized differently, in its conversion with epistemic relations.

The idea of sources as resources does not so much reflect an empirical justification of finding two sources to verify information, for example, but to cover multiple views on a story (i.e., similarities and differences that emerge from source material that does not have to be accessed in person). Hence, an analytical justification of truth is based on the epistemic relation of finding multiple sources to establish truth claims that are not value-free, but if similarities and differences of source material is included, then an analytical truth claim can be established (i.e., an idea of pluralist subjectivity to move toward truth; see table 4.6). Such an undertaking costs time, as sources who provide opposite views may be harder to find than two sources who verify the same information. Bourdieu (1998a) mentioned that time is crucial for critical thinking and the cultural capital of journalism. Power most often is implemented over the control of opinion (Herman and Chomsky, 2002). In the case of economic power, an audience rating way of doing journalism implements power, as Bourdieu (1998a) outlined in his analysis of the emerging model of commercial TV in France. He argued that cultural products such as poetry and literature were never profitable businesses because of their deliberative way of thinking (i.e., a devotion of time). That is a counterargument to a business model of journalism, because the "scoop" is important in journalism.

Table 4.6 Low Social Capital: Epistemic and Social Relations

Epistemic Relation (Analytic Justification of Truth)	Social Relation
"True objectivity is impossible."	"Be fair, value information, and talk to both sides."
"I can't be objective, because objectivity doesn't exist."	"You can be friendly to sources but not [be] friends."
"I know when I have done a good job; I'm my own judge. I like spending a lot of time on a story—I enjoy it; it's my pride."	"Find independent sources; find out where they overlap and what the differences are."
"Trying to get the fairest argument from each side of the conversation. It's my job to pay attention and to move toward the truth and then explain it to my audience."	"Don't be too strongly one part related; be complete. Cover different sources. Give all opinions; it is impossible for journalists to produce value-free stories, because we are all born with a bias, depending on what our backgrounds are or who our parents are."
"You always have to question yourself, and being self-reflective is one of the most important things. Having that kind of rigor and a good editor is most important."	"How can you be honest when you play tennis with the president of the United States? It is not possible."
"We should be a group of disinterested third-party observers who are willing to hold politicians' feet to the fire on both sides of the aisle."	"It is very addictive to be part of the in-group, and you will have to give up your professional distance."

Note: All statements are culled from the qualitative interviews involving correspondents with low access to politicians.

Table 4.6 exemplifies how epistemic relation and social relation may stand in stark contrast under a low social capital condition compared to their relationship under a high social capital condition.

Finding 4: Professional Roles and Justification of Truth

The above findings suggest differences in social capital based on journalists' perceptions of reality. Perceptions of reality influence how journalists interact with sources (i.e., social capital) and how they justify truth (i.e., epistemic relation from knowledge to truth). As a matter of fact, those predictive findings were grounded in the data and hence inductively deduced from the categories. Hence, perceptions of reality based on analytical justification of truth stand in contrast to an empirical justification of truth. In other words, there is a determinal relationship between correspondents who believe to mirror a truth out there, which has to be empirically tested, compared to correspondents who are more likely to approach or move toward truth by embracing a multiperspectival ideal of subjectivity.

The meaning of an empirical justification of truth is conceptually close to a meaning of objectivity that touches on an ontological notion, which "is closely associated with a realistic theory of truth as correspondent with external objects" (Ward, 2009, p. 72). Disagreements of epistemological foundation that implicitly underlie the perception of objectivity are well documented in comparative journalism research (Donsbach and Klett, 1993; Hanitzsch et al., 2011). For example, Donsbach and Klett (1993) surveyed journalists to have them define objectivity in Germany, Great Britain, Italy, and the United States. They found two different professional cultures, the Anglo-Saxon journalists on one side and the continental European journalists on the other side. Donsbach and Klett (1993) referred to two working worlds based on differences in editorial control over news content and differences in role conceptions. Compared to the Anglo-Saxon journalists, objectivity was never a strong professional value for journalists in continental Europe. This may well result from the fact that northern European countries have the highest amount of newspaper readership, whereas in the United States, television plays more of an agenda-setting function (Hallin and Mancini, 2004; Roper, 1985). In other words, the agenda-setting function of a medium may be important to understanding epistemic relations because of their powerful position in the field and their power to define the institutionalized cultural capital of the entire journalism field.

As pointed out earlier, an empirical justification of truth is a strong force for TV journalism, in which viewers trust sound bites and pictures. Thus, if TV journalism is defining the field and setting the agenda, such epistemic relations become important mechanisms defining the entire field. Hence, it is not surprising that objectivity plays an important role in the United States. And it is not surprising that US journalists are more likely to embrace a disseminator role than their foreign colleagues (Tandoc et al., 2013). On the other hand, Hanitzsch et al. (2011) pointed out that journalists in the United States exhibit a tendency to let their own interpretations become part of the story and "that the United States might be no longer been seen as the 'epitome' of an objective journalism" (p. 287). But generalizations are difficult to assess because representative samples of US journalists may not be comparable to political journalists in Washington, DC.

Social perceptions of reality and of the professional ideology of journalism have been widely studied (e.g., Hanitzsch et al., 2011; Weaver et al., 2007), with surveys assessing journalists' conceived roles (i.e., their understanding of their normative tasks as journalists). However, implicit disagreements of epistemological foundations that underlie role conceptions would benefit role conception research to explicate the contradictory forces of mirroring a truth, compared to a ideal of subjectivity.

Such tendencies were thus tested with the survey data to account for differences in justification of truth based on the newly established global understanding of a relationship between access and justification of truth. The results confirm the claim of an objective and ultimate truth out there, which ought to be mirrored, versus the idea of pluralist subjectivity by means of including different voices and analyzing such voices. Although Hanitzsch et al. (2011) found little support among journalists toward providing orientation, the argument here is different; it is based on questions regarding correspondents' practice (i.e., their interaction with sources). Correspondents who embrace a more analytical justification of truth might be more willing to include multicultural voices as a means of providing orientation. The interaction with sources offers an analysis of an evaluative component of journalism (i.e., norms, values, or roles of journalists) explicitly grounded in practice (i.e., in their interaction with sources).

The outputs of truth justification vary, based on perceptions of reality. If journalists empirically "test" a claim, their attempt to influence their audience is significantly stronger than for journalists who apply more of a subjective idea that truth cannot be separated from context and human subjectivity and that the "audience should draw their own conclusion" (foreign correspondent from a low social capital group, personal communication, Washington, DC, January 2012). Hence, an empirical justification of truth is significantly more geared toward an agenda-setting function of a media organization and a rather top-down form of communication.

An interesting aspect in this mixed-methods design is that, based on the findings from the qualitative analysis and the assumption that an empirical justification of truth includes the idea that "true objectivity is possible," a journalist's task to get at the truth also significantly reduces the ideal of keeping a professional distance from the sources (see table 4.7). Correspondents with low access believe more strongly that true objectivity is impossible, whereas correspondents in the high social capital group embrace a task to get at the truth to a significantly higher extent than correspondents with less access to politicians. Furthermore, journalists with high access are significantly more likely to think that it is their job to tell their audiences if a political claim is obviously wrong. In addition, it is also significantly more important for journalists with high access to get the information to the public quickly. High access enables correspondents to more strongly believe that their reporting should influence the opinions of their audiences.

Empirical justification of truth is a stronger force of imposing an agenda over an audience. Empirical truth claims may be stronger

Table 4.7   Professional Roles in Dependence of Social Capital and Access

Input	"I try to maintain a professional distance from my sources."	"My task is to get at the truth."	"True objectivity is impossible."
Low Social Capital	4.08 (0.70)*	4.21 (0.69)**	3.39 (1.05)*
High Social Capital	3.73 (0.94)	4.64 (0.49)	2.87 (1.20)
Output	"I tell my audience if a political claim is obviously wrong."	"It is my job to get information to the public quickly."	"I attempt to produce news stories that influence the opinion of my audience."
Low Social Capital	3.92 (0.84)*	4.06 (0.78)**	2.78 (1.10)*
High Social Capital	4.24 (0.74)	4.41 (0.78)	3.29 (1.23)

* Significant at the .05 level.
** Significant at the .001 level.

epistemologies because of an ideal of an objective perception of truth. Because objectivity has long been established as the gold standard (e.g., Ward, 2009), empirical justification of truth might be a stronger truth claim because of its established normative ideal as being potentially more likely to be converted into institutionalized cultural capital than analytical justification. Here again, the epistemic relation can only be understood from the very specific dynamics of the journalism profession. Truth based on empirical justification is more likely to set the agenda, and journalists articulate such a knowledge more explicitly because they assume that it has stronger cultural capital and that it has high amount of capital that can be exchanged into symbolic capital (when the conversion is based on dialogue and communication; communication as culture) or economic capital (when the conversion is based on monetary value; communication as commerce). Objectivity has been challenged through a technological shift, and because of the economic crisis, traditional media funding models have changed; advertising revenues have been dropping and the media cannot make up for the recent decline in advertising (e.g., Olmstead, Mitchell, and Rosenstiel, 2011).

Whereas objectivity was central to mainstream media in the 20th century, scholars (Christians, 2004; Elliot, 2008; Karlsson, 2010; Singer, 2007) see transparency as an emerging norm, replacing objectivity as a truth-telling strategy. This notably indicates a shift in the institutionalized cultural capital of journalism. It is interesting that forces unleashed by online networks are creating a networked society where objectivity is contested, which indicates a pre-paradigmatic conflict (Hellmueller et al., 2013). Objectivity is contested because "the discourse of professional distance clearly stands in stark contrast to the rhetoric of inclusivity" (Deuze, 2005, p. 456).

The next findings discuss the paradoxical situation that journalists have the opportunity of including content produced by readers, viewers, and participatory journalists, but they, on the other hand, are most likely follow a belief in objectivity while struggling to maintain a professional distance and to defend themselves from new agents transforming their long-established institutionalized cultural capital. These findings are important indicators to understand how forces evoked by a networked society may weaken a long-established institutionalized cultural capital of the field (i.e., objectivity).

In Washington, DC, where journalists are known to hold powerful positions in the field of journalism, as most of them hold long-established reputations as reporters (Willnat and Weaver, 2003), such a change would be particularly powerful because of its high amount of autonomy and hence its privileged position of transforming the cultural capital of the field. Whereas change is most likely to occur with new entrants to a field who are less socialized (Kuhn, 1970), transformation on the autonomous pole is more powerful. Bourdieu applied an Einsteinian physics metaphor to explain how the distribution of capital influences the power of change (see Benson and Neveu, 2005): "The more energy a body has, the more it distorts the space around it, and a very powerful agent within a field can distort the whole space, cause the whole space to be organized in relation to itself" (p. 43). In other words, the more a reporter is established and autonomous, the more power he or she has to change the space to be organized in relation to its intended direction of change.

Finding 5: Digital Networked Conversation?

Are Journalists Joining the Conversation, or Are Participants Joining the Journalistic Conversation?

> I still think that, like in any professional relationship, technology can definitely help a great deal, but at the end, the personal face-to-face relationship is still the most valuable and useful relation among human beings. (US correspondent, personal communication, Washington, DC, January 13, 2012)

Twitter has become a regular part of daily news. This poses two challenges for journalists. First, they have to decide whether they want or are able to join the Twitter conversation. Furthermore, are correspondents letting those sources join their journalistic conversation? Here again, the focus of investigation was to look at how that may change the social capital of journalists. Have access and face-to-face contact been replaced by forms of computer-mediated communication? How does this transform the social capital of journalists with less access to politicians? Do forms of computer-mediated communication provide a more egalitarian form of a reporter-source relationship? Because information is linked in a networked society, how has that shifted journalism's focus from pitching for the scoop to a more egalitarian form of sharing information since, in the 24-hour news cycle, a scoop may not last too long?

How the new digital landscape will transform the work in Washington, DC is considered the "one-billion dollar question" (foreign correspondent of low social capital, personal communication, Washington, DC, January 2012). For long-established journalists (high social capital), it seems clear that "my news organization is an established source and would not accept a non-professional journalist and we have our rules. You take stories from *The New York Times* for granted, but bloggers write what they want." Correspondents in DC distinguish themselves from citizen or participatory journalists by referring to participatory journalists' lack of professionalism: "CNN iReporters, for example; for a real professional, it means nothing. It is dangerous, because there is no control." The main concern here is for correspondents to draw a line between them and the "others": "Anybody can report on things; anybody can have a blog. Some blogs are great. But there is a real discipline to the practice as it is the case of any profession. Just because you have a platform does not mean you know the content" (US correspondents of low social capital, personal communication, Washington, DC, January 2012).

Other correspondents are less pessimistic and use Twitter as a headline feed, for example: "I also follow good, smart reporters. Sometimes you see news breaking on Twitter. You have to follow them. It's basically just another source of information" (US correspondent of low social capital, personal communication, Washington, DC, January 2012).

Or as another correspondent (foreign, low social capital) pointed out: "I appreciate the positive development of gaining more sources, to get an idea of a story; you can begin a relationship, but you cannot establish a relationship." On the other hand, "you want to be differentiated from online news; otherwise, everyone gets their news online" (foreign correspondent, medium social capital). Some correspondents attribute the crisis in journalism to the new entrants in the journalism field: "The crisis we have is because of the bloggers. I do not think they should be considered journalists. Journalists have tools and skills and a commitment to the truth" (foreign correspondent, medium social capital). Nevertheless, correspondents used Twitter as a top-down communication channel to "post my stories and to receive feedback because you are so far away" (foreign correspondent, medium social capital). For some older generations of journalists working in Washington, DC, social media disturbs them because "they compromise journalistic ethics, like objectivity and truthfulness." Traditional myths such as objectivity remain important weapons to defend the journalistic field against new entrants. One US correspondent was very cynical in evaluating computer-mediated relationships:

> The internet is like mental masturbation. I do not think it can replace human contact. If it does, we are no longer considered humans. It dehumanizes and desensitizes people to kill people, with video games,

for example. But I do not want us to become like that. If we become dehumanized, we lose our collective soul. (Personal communication, Washington, DC, January 2012)

To summarize, US and foreign correspondents both agreed on the potential danger of participatory journalism to diminish journalism's commitment to the truth. These findings are consistent with the literature on journalism and social media. A project by the Pew Research Center's Project for Excellence in Journalism and the George Washington University's School of Media and Public Affairs analyzed how 13 major news organizations use Twitter feeds and found that Twitter is used in limited ways in journalism (Holcomb, Gross, and Mitchell, 2011). Most often, Twitter is used as an added means to disseminate the organization's material, matching very closely the news events on the news organizations' legacy platforms. Singer (2005) argued that print-based routines remain salient in an online setting. The culture of newsroom, the "we write, you read" mentality of modern journalism, remains visible: "One of the most fundamental 'truths' in journalism…the professional journalist is the one who determines what publics see, hear and read about the world" (Deuze, 2005, p. 451). Lewis, Kaufhold, and Lasorsa (2010) have elaborated on how community newspaper editors embrace the challenge of institutionalizing digital media into daily reporting routines. Their findings point to the more obvious conclusion that "community newspaper editors have widely different opinions about and rationales for rebuffing or embracing citizen journalism" (p. 176). If they embraced citizen journalism, contributors were carefully selected for their expertise and were still subject to an editor's review.

If bloggers are considered players in the field of journalism, then the pressure from the political field becomes stronger to control and influence them because politicians can themselves control the journalistic conversation. The interviewed correspondents reinforced an argument outlined in the literature review: if journalists advocate for society, and if a democracy gets to hold journalists responsible for their work or if their work is based on self-regulation, then there needs to be criteria on how to evaluate the democratic function in different formations of democracies of media (e.g., Baker, 2002). With new entrants, such criteria are up for negotiation, which creates uncertainty and with it a potential danger for journalism as a social institution if journalism is moving toward a societal conversation as part of other fields but without its unique cultural capital.

Finding 6: Reconstructing Social and Epistemic Relations

The four quadrants in table 4.8 summarize the conversion rate between cultural and social capital. However, the table should not mislead to the conclusion that all correspondents fit into one of the four quadrants. Membership in one quadrant is not mutually exclusive to another one. Journalists' truth claims can shift with a generational turnover, or "pressure from neighboring fields" (Benson and Neveu, 2005, p. 6) can transform the cultural capital. Such a change is most likely to happen if truth claims are no longer being trusted. In other words, if politicians are no longer willing to provide information to news organizations, or if audiences are no longer willing to consume particular news, trust is re-established by a transformation of the cultural capital. In the objectivity era, to trust in news meant to rely on a source, which required no further inquiry. While objectivity functioned as a trust regulator, audiences trusted in journalists' accuracy of depictions, in the journalists' assessment, in the selectivity of topics, and in the selectivity of facts. Now combined with a technological shift, such a trust behavior has shifted so that the open access network enables people to see behind trust mechanisms. In a certain way, new technologies have the potential to educate the audience about trust mechanisms. The internet has the potential to emancipate audiences to have more knowledge about journalists' assessments, selectivity, and

Table 4.8   Positive and Negative Conversions of Social Capital into Cultural Capital

Conversion of Social Capital into Cultural Capital +	
• Evidence and experience on the ground	• Variety of sources
• Truth is "in" the source/facts	• Self-reflective
• Closeness to a source	• Truth is independent from sources/ facts
• True objectivity is important	• Professional distance to a source
• Organizational procedure	• Moving toward truth and objectivity
• Adherence to organizational rules	• Time importance, independence
• Adherence to source rules	• Analytical knowledge
• Empirical knowledge	
• Falsification	
Empirical Justification	**Analytical Justification**
• Professional distance to source	• Closeness to a source
• Lack of organizational procedures, lack of organizational trust	• Lack of reflexivity
	• Personal bias
Conversion of Social Capital into Cultural Capital –	

accuracy of depictions, so trust does not necessarily start with the news organization; it goes beyond. In a way, journalism is struggling for a redefinition of its normative role. Weinberger (2009) therefore called for a shift to transparency as the new objectivity. Transparency is the new objectivity because it still serves the same purpose—it enhances reliability. Therefore, the added value is for journalists to let people see behind the process and enhance knowledge on the final draft's claims and the ideas that informed it.

The quadrants in table 4.8 exemplify the mutual exclusiveness of such a final draft's claims, which include the conversion rate between cultural and social capital. Without doubt, social capital is one of the most important cornerstones of political journalism—if not the most important—and correspondents spend time thinking about how to interact with their sources and how to report about them, how to build professional relationships with sources, and what "professional relationships" imply. Their answers reveal sophisticated and reflective statements on how a relationship with a source can be justified from within the profession. The two poles of empirical and analytical justification reinforce two opposite epistemic relations, which become implicit guidelines that determine truth but are hardly ever articulated. The two poles embody tacit knowledge of professional tasks, knowledge of an epistemic relation that is not always known explicitly but is embedded in routines through which truth claims naturalize themselves. An empirical justification motivates experience and evidence as a basis for truth claims. Relationships with sources are based on closeness to a source, to empirically test knowledge, because of the source's inherent dependence on truth (i.e., the "truth is in the source"; foreign correspondent, high social capital). On the other end, on the analytical justification of truth's end, closeness to source is evaluated as diminishing epistemic relations between knowledge and truth because of its belief in truth being independent from sources and a professional distance being important to a move toward truth.

Another reason for a sophisticated aspect of evaluative level of social capital stems from the fact that correspondents have spent some time in the profession; they are well-socialized into a "game logic" of journalism and they have had to articulate their tacit knowledge more frequently than newcomers. Meanwhile, because of their experiences, they feel responsible to safeguard the gates, not only the gates of information and the gates of sources, but also the gates of the field. New entrants such as bloggers are still very much perceived to be a disruptive force, which transforms the profession into an uncertain entity in which an outcome of a shared understanding of what constitutes journalism in a few years is not yet known. Dealing with uncertainties thus forces journalists to rethink their positions and to reconsider their normative roles in society. Hence, such a renegotiation of truth-telling strategies may move the profession toward an in-depth understanding of what constitutes the field of journalism, by explicating tacit knowledge that determines the practical task of how journalists construct truth.

5

The DC Transnational Journalism Culture of the 21st Century

Journalists who are stars are Bigfoots who walk into a room and politicians would come to them. The problem with being a Bigfoot is that you always end up reporting the main story. And often, the main story is not the real story. The real story is that everybody knows Mitt Romney will lose. The real story is that we are in a period of an economic crisis. Well, that is harder to cover than the primaries. And it is not just an American story—it's a German, a Swiss story, and we still do not cover the real story; we only cover bits of it. But I found that if you cover the real story, you often find the greater truth.

—US correspondent, personal communication,
Washington, DC, January 2012

The prevalence of digital technologies has shifted journalists' relations with sources and highlighted the tensions that the profession had faced for so many years: How close can journalists position themselves to their sources? Should a journalist become a "Bigfoot," or would that affect reporting on sources? How is control negotiated over a professional distance to sources? This relationship with sources affects news content, and relationships become more complex in a transnational news environment. To provide an explanation for this phenomenon, this chapter first summarizes the most important findings from the mixed-method analysis of a sourcing culture in Washington, DC. Those findings together then provide insight into the source-reporter relationship in the 21st century and have implications for journalism education and journalism theories.

The quantitative surveys as well as the qualitative interviews of this book reveal how cognitive and evaluative structures of journalism culture are permeated through practice (i.e., the performative level). In a way, the performative level is the most immediate to people, as they can witness news content every day. However, people are not able to always see what journalists think when they perform their job or which norms are guiding their news-gathering behavior. This fourth chapter brings together the findings from the first, second, and third chapters and discusses the implications of the findings in regard to journalism education and journalism theory.

First, the web survey assessed journalists' perceptions of their political sources. Source credibility and perceived homophily were investigated in a transnational journalism environment to understand how the cognitive level of journalism culture (perception, attitudes, and news judgments of journalists) shape a transnational journalism culture. The survey integrated other forces, such as gatekeeping constraints, that affect the work of DC correspondents. This first cognitive level of news gathering in a transnational news environment explains how journalists perceive their sources: "It is by studying how journalists from all walks of their professional life negotiate the core values that one can see the occupational ideology of journalism at work" (Deuze, 2005, p. 458).

The main focus of both empirical studies was to investigate how correspondents do their work based on their positions in the field (i.e., based on their social closeness to their sources). What are their methods of reporting and their use of news formats if they share similar values and ideas with politicians? The perceptions and interpretations of news (i.e., the cognitive level; Hanitzsch, 2007a) is embedded in what journalists do (i.e., the performative level of a journalism culture). This study examined perceptions to explain performance because "Journalists—mostly unconsciously—perpetuate these deep structures through professional performance" (Hanitzsch, 2007a, p. 369). In carrying out the study, particular attention was paid to linking perceptions to performance by explicitly asking correspondents about their most recent news story.

Social Capital: Sources as Journalists' Precious Resources

Social capital in a journalism field was conceptualized according to the web survey findings. In a networked sourcing environment, relationships with sources become more salient and integral part of journalists' routines. Hence, journalists are drawn by necessity into relationships with sources. However, in a way, this concept of closeness to a source is contradictory to the professional claim of autonomy of being detached and impartial. The focus of interest was to investigate social capital in a journalistic field. Social capital was conceptualized according to Bourdieu (1986) as actual or potential resources of institutionalized relationship of mutual acquaintance and recognition. Recognition specified in a journalistic field is rooted in the complex undercurrents of the field's professional ideology: Under what conditions do journalists evaluate relationships with politicians as beneficial—as a social capital and potential resource to be converted into trust and symbolic capital among audiences? One major concern was to explicate collaborative autonomy as a unique journalistic concept in a field where openness remained the core ideal of the field for many decades. Journalists draw on existing social structures determined by the amount of resources the media organization has, how much they are influenced by the political field, and how much they let the audience participate in the news-construction process. Journalists also reproduce the existing social structure through their professional tasks. Thus, institutionalized social capital serves to uphold the status quo of the reporter's position in the field.

Journalists are players in a field of social networks where much of what is supposed to be "fit to print" is selected based on social relationships and truth claims: "What fits [has] got to be true" (US correspondent, personal communication, Washington, DC, January 11, 2012). US and foreign correspondents in Washington, DC are political junkies who might become addicted to getting close to politicians, becoming Bigfoot, and socializing with political sources, because of the importance of gaining firsthand information. On the other hand, the danger of reporting the source's viewpoint instead of reporting the news has been well documented. For example, if politicians are interested in preserving their political power, then minimizing the professional distance between journalists and sources can lead journalists to report everything politicians tell them (US correspondent, personal communication, Washington, DC, January 12, 2012). Journalistic credibility and its potential symbolic capital are jeopardized if journalists give up their professional distance (Tuchman, 1978).

The annual White House dinner is indicative of journalists socializing with politicians in Washington, DC. Some correspondents have become cynical about the event:

At the White House correspondents' dinner, I would always have a table, but I would invite people who had been a real help—secretary, staff people. I would always take secretaries to reward them for being helpful during that year. However, things have changed. The dinner has now become a circus, where you bring movie stars, celebrity guests, to tell the world, "Look at me; I can bring the cast from XY." So I stopped going. You [as a journalist] are not supposed to go into the field but to stand on the sidelines. (US correspondent, personal communication, Washington, DC, January 11, 2012)

The journalistic role conception of being independent and standing on the sidelines has been contested. After the Watergate scandal, many newspapers embraced a critical attitude toward politicians and an adversarial journalistic role conception evolved (Weaver et al., 2007). In essence, it became very fashionable to attempt to bring a president down, if a journalist wanted to succeed in his or her career (US correspondent, personal communication, Washington, DC, January 12, 2012). However, as Hanitzsch et al. (2011) pointed out in their comparative journalism research, there is an emerging tendency in the United States of journalists letting their own interpretation become part of the story. Journalists are not necessarily embracing a critical role toward politicians but instead are enforcing their own predispositions (also see Donsbach, 2004). Hanitzsch et al. (2011) concluded that "the United States might be no longer been seen as the 'epitome' of an objective journalism" (p. 287). Hence, this research sets out to investigate how journalists' perceptions of politicians and social relations between correspondents and politicians shape correspondents' work in DC—in a contemporary, transnational, 21st-century journalism field. In a way, this book is also providing evidence to a still existing variety of journalism cultures, surviving and redefining themselves in the technological circumstances of the 21st century. And while new news-gathering practices are emerging, such as participatory forms of the CNN iReporter, journalism is still very much defined by the three levels of journalism culture (i.e., the cognitive, performative, and evaluative levels).

Being Close versus Being Objective

It is not news in the 21st century that journalists are drawn into relationships with sources based on the nature of their job—that is, to inform the public based on information gained from sources. However, journalists' professional ideologies and their normative strategies represent a counterforce to the closeness to sources as being detached, objective, and impartial. The negotiation process of this paradoxical situation is what has changed in the 21st century. On one hand, journalists are interacting with sources in various ways (ranging from social networks to face-to-face communication) and getting close to them to gather information for their audiences. On the other hand, journalists must be balanced and detached from sources—these are synonymous keywords that indicate a journalist's relationship with sources based on a continuing need for the verification of truth. There is a self-regulative element in the field of journalism and journalists are well aware of "a professional distance to sources." For example, Connie Schultz, a Pulitzer Prize–winning columnist stepped down from her position, citing a conflict of interest at the *Cleveland Plain Dealer* when her husband, Senator Sherrod Brown (D-Ohio), sought re-election (Terkel, 2012).

However, on July 9, 2012, Schultz received an e-mail from a blogger, in which her closeness to the source she was supposed to cover was criticized. The blogger was not aware of the fact that she was married to the senator:

> We are doing an exposé on journalists in the elite media who socialize with elected officials they are assigned to cover. We have found numerous photos of you with Sen. Sherrod Brown. In one of them, you appear to be hugging him. Care to comment? (Terkel, 2012)

Hence, this research shed light on exactly the question of what are the consequences of her reporting if Schultz is married to Senator Brown? What does it entail if a source is socially close to the journalist? How can journalists maintain their autonomy, and how is such an understanding of autonomy culturally determined by the field in question (i.e., the field of journalism)?

The threefold purpose of this research matters, because without deconstructing journalism culture in its elements and applying a heuristic framework (i.e., Hanitzsch, 2007a) to categorize findings, important aspects of a journalism culture remain in the dark. Foremost, journalism research has long implicitly accepted an unexplained gap between the evaluative element (what journalism ought to be) and its respective performance (i.e., how journalism is performed) by studying one element and referring to another element in its conclusion.

For example, the Worlds of Journalism study project rests on the normative assumption that there is a close connection between journalists' role conceptions and media content (Hanitzsch et al., 2011;

Patterson and Donsbach, 1996; Starck and Soloski, 1977). The project surveys journalists across 80 countries and argues that this role conception will eventually shape their behavior on their job (Hanitzsch, 2011). However, there exists mounting empirical evidence that journalists' practical constraints may influence the assumed linear relationship between their role conception and their job performance. Hence, this assumed overlap of practice and norm should be questioned rather than presumed (Tandoc, Hellmueller, and Vos, 2013). This book sets the framework for approaching journalism culture by combining those levels. This book also provides an understanding of influences over journalism culture and the way to analytically distinguish between the three levels of transnational journalism culture. On the other hand, it highlights the importance of approaching journalism culture from an intercultural communication theoretical framework to pick up on many nuances of correspondents' background and personal experiences, which might be overlooked when studying journalists as a representative of their nation only. There will appear a more nuanced view of journalists working in a transnational environment if we approach the research inquiry from an intercultural communication theoretical framework.

Intercultural Communication Approach

The results emphasize the importance of examining interpersonal communication between sources and journalists by applying intercultural communication variables. As pointed out in the introduction, a networked society enhances interactions with various sources of information. In a networked society, interactions and relationships with other information providers become salient. Singer (2007) argued that with journalism becoming increasingly deinstitutionalized, the role of the reporter becomes more important than ever before. How journalists interact with sources and how they are connected increase in significance, shifting away from studying discrete products and functions of journalists. Particularly, in a network environment, "no single message is discrete; all messages connect to each other" (Singer, 2010, p. 118).

A Network Environment of News Gathering

Such a network environment contributes to a higher potential of being connected across countries to a variety of people and in journalists' case, to a variety of news sources. Digital technologies enable inexpensive and fast communication across the globe, so communication effectiveness may no longer only be explained by a country-of-origin variable. In fact, findings from previous intercultural communication studies (J. C. McCroskey and Teven, 1999; L. L. McCroskey, 2002, 2003; Teven, 2008) were supported. Journalists perceive politicians to be more trustworthy, more caring about the public, and more competent if they perceive them as sharing their attitudes or perceive politicians' backgrounds to be similar to their own. Social relations are important in shaping correspondents' perceptions of source credibility. The relationship between source credibility and perceived homophily holds true for both US and foreign correspondents. In essence, intercultural communication variables are better predictors of perceived source credibility than country-of-origin variables.

The Communication Setting in the 21st Century

Face-to-face interactions and personal forms of communication remain important for categorizing a source as belonging to the in-group or the out-group (Ho and McLeod, 2008). The working environment influences the manifestations of perceptions: perceptions of attitude homophily significantly predicted all three dimensions of source credibility for journalists who had personal contact with their sources. Hence, Donsbach's (2004) argument can be extended to different communication contexts: Quasi-objectifying strategies of journalists based on external or internal forces (such as other media or the opinion of correspondents' editor) when selecting news are stronger when fewer social clues are involved and when journalists have less autonomy in defining the valence of sources. On the other hand, quasi-objectifying strategies or the influence of other variables than the journalists' perception are less important the more autonomy a journalist holds. Furthermore, this study found support for Benson and Neveu's (2005) explanation in line with Bourdieu's argument that "the more energy a body has, the more it distorts the space around it" (p. 43). Journalists who possess more autonomy are more likely to organize the journalism field in relation to themselves to define the quasi-objective criteria. Positions in the journalistic field do not explain what information passes through the gate (e.g., Lewin, 1947; Shoemaker and Vos, 2009) but rather how information from sources passes through the gate. For example, how journalists interact with sources can explain whether or not perception matters for the news coverage. Although Gatekeeping Theory is mostly interested in what passes through and what is left out, field positions are better predictors of how news items pass through the gate and how constraints on the levels of influence limit the practice of journalists, both of which are important in understanding attempts to build frames and valence that are inherent in news reports.

The Unique Dynamic of the Journalism Field

The findings point to the importance of considering journalism theories when studying journalists' perceptions of politicians to account for the unique dynamic of the journalism profession. A comprehensive understanding of how to grasp autonomy in a journalism field is an undertaking that certainly needs more scholarly attention. According to Bourdieu (1998a), journalists' autonomy is high where external influence is low. When journalists' autonomy is high, journalists are more likely to embrace the disseminator or detached watchdog role (Hanitzsch, 2011). Furthermore, autonomy from a journalist's perspective is understood as having influence over one's own work. In essence, correspondents believe that their own experiences should have an influence on their stories. This is not surprising, as journalists are the ones constructing the news, and denying their efforts would be denying the importance of their work to perform a journalistic task. However, journalists who embrace the disseminator role are more likely to judge politicians' credibility based on their perceived attitude similarity with them. Hence, it may well be that control over one's story implies reinforcing one's viewpoint in a news report.

Journalism scholars and journalism educators should ask what meaning is implied if the large-scope aim is journalistic autonomy, which—according to the findings of this study—eventually contributes to the visibility of journalists' viewpoints in news outputs. Powerful sources may impose a media agenda due to their powerful position by reinforcing journalists' viewpoints because politicians have visibility in society and resources to communicate to a mass audience. However, a journalism and political culture suitable to a self-governing society is serving an audience that is more fragmented than ever before. Hence, multiculturalism becomes an important practical inquiry along with its established professional ideology (e.g., Deuze, 2005). Reinforcing politicians' viewpoints in news outputs may neglect such multicultural claims.

How Objective Are Journalists?

The qualitative interviews highlight an inconsistency between evaluative and performative elements of journalism. Journalists expressed a struggle in rationalizing what journalism ought to be, what they would like to do, and what they eventually end up reporting. For example, all the interviewed journalists for this study referred to an ideal type of objectivity, regardless of whether correspondents were socialized in the United States. However, how journalists apply objectivity in practice differs based on the medium, correspondents' experience in DC, access to sources, and other cultural dimensions. It is clear that correspondents conceptualize objectivity as being something abstract, something that needs clarification and practical elaboration, and something that requires meaning. Objectivity is mentioned in context and not as a stand-alone word: "We have to try to be objective. Ah, a magic word. What does it mean?" (foreign correspondent, personal communication, Washington, DC, January 13, 2012) or "The main goal is objectivity, but how objective can a person be? That is the main question" (foreign correspondent, personal communication, Washington, DC, January 14, 2012). Objectivity, as defined by US and foreign correspondents in Washington, DC, is a "word in context" and does not reveal its merit in itself. That makes it socially powerful, because a socially defined meaning can objectify the meaning of it and legitimize its judgment based on that meaning (e.g., "a journalist can only be objective by not playing golf with a politicians," or "a journalist can only be objective by constantly questioning her own opinion").

The objectivity norm exists as a platform of an ongoing battle serving a purpose of critical engagement with the normative ideal of journalism and a form of social power in its legitimization. In a way, by talking, thinking, or criticizing a norm, journalists and scholars have to produce a reflexive knowledge of the norm (i.e., the underlying assumptions that apply to judgment of normative behaviors), which enables journalism as a field to foster a deeper understanding of a constitutive normative role of the media (i.e., what journalism can do, how it affects the public, and what it ought to provide for a self-governing society). Such battles over redefinitions of objectivity have challenged roles of journalists in a way that they shed light on what function journalists should serve (e.g., is it my task to get at the truth or to mirror reality?) and how such a task should be performed (actively involved or detached?).

An objective news report is more likely to be accepted by today's media audiences than a news report that lacks objective reporting. Objectivity can regulate trust and enhance the public's reliance on information, a normative agreement that enables the public to trust certain kind of information (Weinberger, 2009), which provides the basis for media's recognition: "If people trust your company, then you are good" (foreign correspondent, personal communication, Washington, DC, January 13, 2012). Furthermore, journalists strive to enhance credibility among media audiences to contribute to a deliberative discussion in society: "You have to be objective and realize the truth" because "when you are quoting second-hand information, you do not have the credibility, because the viewer is trusting someone on the ground more than someone who is not there" (foreign correspondent, Washington, DC, personal communication, January 2012).

Technological Changes Affecting Normative Ideals

Challenged with a technological change in journalism, scholarly work has certainly accomplished much to foster understanding of how to conceptualize objectivity. For example, media ethics scholar Ward (2009) redefined objectivity by re-establishing its multidimensional meanings and the different values attached to them. A normative theory of journalism in Ward's sense is "a judicious blend of the romantic and objective impulse" (p. 80). In that sense, the romantic impulse is a passion for interesting interpretations; the objective impulse is a passion for justified interpretations. Ward's focus is a need to develop a more adequate epistemology of journalism, a reformed theory of objectivity that changes the practice of journalism in terms of how stories are constructed and evaluated. This reflects a long-needed questioning of assumptions in journalism research: How do people come to claim something to be true? Indeed, studying the news-construction process reveals justification processes based on journalists' beliefs of what constitutes truth.

From Knowledge to Truth

In fact, an understanding of how journalists construct truth provides a practically adequate and epistemologically based understanding of a transnational journalism culture. In essence, journalism as a knowledge institution bases its knowledge on the truth claim that journalists' first obligation is to the truth (Kovach and Rosenstiel, 2001).

People know they have certain knowledge about something, but they are sometimes not quite sure how they came to know a certain thing. For example, they may know various stories about how the global banking scandal may affect the investigation of possible crimes or which bank might be facing a fine next for its "involvement in manipulating the key lending rate between banks" (Slater and

Jones, 2012). But there is a qualitative distinction between knowledge claims and truth: Truth is based on the notion that some knowledge claims can be considered more epistemologically powerful than others (Maton, 2003). Knowledge claims may elicit truth. They transform into truths through their interpretation and their justification as part of the epistemic relation between knowledge and truth. In other words, people can be aware that the global banking scandal may affect the investigation of possible crimes, but they may doubt its truthfulness. Hence, people abstract it through a method of justification to objectify it as true or not (e.g., by quoting a variety of sources all referring to the same development). A truth claim becomes more powerful than pure knowledge because of its transformation in where truth legitimatized itself; it has been tested or achieved. The investment is the implicit conversion into its truth format. Epistemological relativism is interested in such collective procedures through which judgments are produced. Maton (2003) argued for a reflexivity that is collective rather than individualistic, procedural rather than narcissist. When actors make knowledge claims or engage in practices, they are making a claim of legitimacy for those practices.

The qualitative interviews reveal empirical justification of truth as the stronger force of imposing an agenda over an audience. Indeed, empirical truth claims may be stronger epistemologies because of an ideal of an objective perception of truth (Ward, 2009). Empirical justification of truth may be a stronger truth claim because of its finalized form of truth. From an analytical justification of truth standpoint, truth is still negotiable because of the absence of a final stage of truth—that is, it does not have an end in itself, whereas empirical justifications have ends in themselves; there is no more to say than that truth has been tested.

Reconstructing Journalism's Multicultural Capital

One advantage of combining the performative level with the evaluative and cognitive levels is that scholarly discourses are combined. Journalism culture is "a fast-changing object of inquiry" (Hanitzsch, 2007a, p. 371), and hence, studying its multiple facets requires grasping journalism culture more holistically and conceptualizing definitions that are more likely to be consistent over time.

This study integrated a grounded theory approach to provide new knowledge to the study of transnational journalism culture. It is generally acknowledged that grounded theorists create theory, but what kinds of theories and under what understanding of a theory? From a positivist definition of theory, theoretical concepts are variables, from which we operationalize the empirical definition to test. The idea is to achieve explanation and prediction. On the other hand, a rather interpretive definition of theory aims at understanding rather than explaining: "Proponents of this definition view theoretical understanding as abstract and interpretive; the very understanding gained from the theory rests on the theorist's interpretation of the studied phenomenon" (Charmaz, 2006, p. 126). Grounded theory analyses show patterns and connections rather than linear reasoning. From the standpoint of interpretive theory, facts and values are inextricably linked. This study reconstructed journalism multicultural capital by applying the two theory-building ideas. The results based on the web survey shed light on explanations and predictions of valence of political sources in news based on social positions of correspondents. Furthermore, the qualitative interviews offered a thick description of patterns and connections between the social and cultural capital of the journalistic field. Hence, the qualitative analysis revealed variations in conversion strategies based on analytical and empirical justification of truth. It may well be that such a variation in sourcing practices was evident in this analysis because by keeping source interaction constant in a way that the structure of the field is set, correspondents carry with them a form of institutionalized capital transformed based on their embodied cultural capital.

In line with this argument, it does not seem surprising that one of the correspondents reporting for a French audience revealed strong support for an analytical justification of truth. While a global media culture is emerging that closely resembles the Liberal Model (e.g., Hallin and Mancini, 2004), this case demonstrates adherence to an interpretive or literary style of journalism, which is an element of the French journalism culture (Hallin and Mancini, 2004). The combined results of the empirical studies show how journalists' interaction (i.e., performative part of a journalism culture) with sources is an expression of their truth-telling justification (i.e., evaluative category).

Furthermore, correspondents are aware that there exists a gap between how they think their profession ought to be and how they evaluate their practice as it is. Hence, the evaluative dimension can be considered to comprise of an evaluative dimension explicating a rather normative abstraction of how it should be and the day-by-day experiences of how journalism is practiced. The pressure of economic capital has particularly come as a negative consequence in that journalists cannot always follow what they might think is ethically right: "It happens quite often that sources now tell you they will only answer your questions if you pay them" (foreign correspondent, personal communication, Washington DC, January, 2012). In response to what correspondents think journalism ought to be, the answer was as follows: "As romance had it, we should be a group of disinterested third-party observers who are willing to hold politicians' feet to the fire on both sides on the aisle. But again, we are too busy covering Justin Bieber."

The Question We Ask; the Answers We Get

By reconstructing journalism culture, it becomes evident that if scholars ask journalists normative questions, it is not possible to hold them accountable for their responses. In the largest comparative journalism research to date, Hanitzsch and his collaborators in 18 countries (Hanitzsch et al., 2011), which will be expanded to 80 countries in an ongoing research project, asked journalists about their role conceptions (i.e., their institutional role). In their questionnaire, they included the following question to measure institutional roles of journalists: "The following list describes some of the things the news media do or try to do. Please tell me on a scale of 1 to 5 how important is each of these things in your work" (see Worlds of Journalisms Project, 2007). Here, an ambiguity occurs because surveyed journalists could either answer this question on a normative level (i.e., this thing is very important in my work as part of my professional ideology, but newsroom constraints neglect the importance of such roles) or on a more practical level (e.g., this thing is important because my newsroom encourages this role). Eventually, for scholars interested in whether roles will translate into news output categories, such distinctions are not of small scale. In the first case, roles are not necessarily manifested in news, whereas in the second case, roles are embedded in practice. Survey questions are more reliable if we explicitly refer to only one idea of role conception. An example applied in this research is to refer to journalists' last news story. Such a question wording enhances the construct validity of role conception. If we are interested in role conception on a normative level, then the question can be about their truth-telling strategies or how much influence this thing should have. It may well be that both levels reveal similar answers. This is particularly important to know because in journalism research surveys, responses on role conceptions are assumed to transform into journalistic news outputs. However, such assumptions are vulnerable to a normative bridge (i.e., norms should guide the profession) and to the question of how reliable journalists' answers are, referring to the problem of socially desirable answers in surveys (i.e., are they really revealing how they do journalism?).

Implication for Journalism Education

This empirical study has important consequences when thinking about journalism education. Enhancing journalism students' awareness of their own positions (their backgrounds and resources) could greatly benefit by shifting the education away from a particularly normative focus to understand tacit knowledge (such as objectivity) embedded in journalistic practices.

Furthermore, in a transnational context, various cultures are intertwined, negotiated, and can be understood by social relations that determine how correspondents perceive politicians. If we are interested in how media messages develop, then applying intercultural communication theories provide a better theoretical framework than comparing normative ideals across countries and interpreting results based on the country variable, by pointing out that differences exist because of countries' cultures. The country is not supposed to be the force in intercultural communication research, but the position and perception of how close agents stand to each other offers valuable findings for understanding sourcing in a transnational journalism environment. Groups that are perceived to be socially similar—such as teenagers, academics, or journalists—may share more similarities across countries than different social groups within one country (de Mooij, 2010).

In addition, this is important because social positions shape valence frames of politicians. As this study revealed, background homophily and goodwill are significant predictors of valence. This is consistent with previous studies. For example, Teven (2008) found goodwill to be the strongest predictor of candidate believability. Politicians who interact more with their voters are more likely to be perceived as credible and thus more favorable news frames emerge from such social perceptions.

Educating journalists about their epistemologies is best done at an early stage so that such invisible structures can be understood before their first job. This shows the early legitimatization of such cultural capital at journalism schools: "If students are continually exposed to and educated about the importance of understanding race, class and culture, it will become second nature. It will become a natural part of the journalism they produce" (Perry, 2006, p. 11).

Hierarchy of Experiences in the Newsroom

The capacity to perform journalism is transforming established hierarchies in newsrooms. Journalists trained in multimedia and convergence storytelling are digital natives, and they possess skills applicable to a digital newsroom environment, something that veteran journalists have had to learn on the job. Hence, the hierarchy of experiences is shifting. Senior journalists may no longer be the ones embodying more experiences in journalistic skills than junior journalists. In addition, junior journalists are no longer necessarily trained by older journalists as was the case for many decades (e.g., Darnton, 1975), where adherence to the established practices and norms would eventually determine their position in the hierarchy. What underlies this problematic shift in control over journalistic knowledge is the "consensus among practitioners that the status quo in the industry is the ideal one; hence, newcomers only need to internalize what their senior peers already do" (Deuze, 2006a, p. 21). Negotiating hierarchy positions poses two problems to the industry and the education of journalists-to-be. The media industry might be particularly interested in hiring multimedia journalists who possess a particular skill set. Such expectations put pressure on universities to place a strong focus on skills classes. However, "university education must construct a broader professionalism of civic engagement if students are to contribute effectively to a democratic society" (Reese, 2001, p. 175). Practical journalistic skills and civic engagement are intertwined, and journalists' training should involve both: learning news-gathering practices that benefit a multicultural society and enhancing civic engagement by critical thinking. Shoemaker (1993) argued that critical thinking represents a cornerstone of any journalism education. Critical thinking has become a buzzword—however, it should not be confused with embracing an adversarial journalistic role. Critical thinking involves the process of reasoning and reflecting, thinking well and fair mindedly not just about one's own beliefs but also challenging and identifying assumptions and understandings that human actions and thoughts are grounded in a specific context (Shoemaker, 1993). Critical thinking is particularly important in a multicultural context where assumptions about people's behavior are rooted in historical and cultural contexts and function as invisible guidelines of a person's tacit knowledge. Trying to explore alternatives of a journalist's first approach to a story may enhance understanding of a situation where absolute answers are not the final product. The final product is the ambiguity that, without the critical-thinking processes, presumes an absolute answer because of a dualism ideal (i.e., that there exists a right or wrong answer).

Critical-Thinking Skills

While witnessing a growing multicultural movement that is transforming newsrooms and working conditions of journalists, this research proceeds to provide practical and normative implications of how to enhance critical-thinking skills among current and future journalists to foster an understanding of sourcing in a multicultural environment. This is important because multiculturalism serves a contemporary professional ideology embedded in every journalist's routine decision making. How can this research contribute to the education of global journalism? Journalism education literature tends to be highly normative or overtly descriptive (Deuze, 2006a). This debate has been structurally embedded in journalism education and training from the beginning of the twentieth century and is thus socially powerful. However, the issue could be approached by "dissolving the perceived dichotomy between theory and practice" (Deuze, 2006a, p. 22). In doing so, research can then "take responsibility for [our] findings when studying the work of journalists" (Deuze, 2006a, p. 31).

Many paths lead to Rome, but journalism curriculum can certainly profit from research on how critical thinking can be enhanced by understanding one's position in a field of power—in a field of social and epistemic relations with potential sources of journalistic news. Journalism is information coupled with a truth claim. Such truth claims are important because they explain how information becomes journalistically justified and, as such, a socially powerful strategic piece of news that creates distinctions in society and may lead to institutional biases in cases where truth claims naturalize themselves, where they become embedded in journalistic routines.

Journalism has long been plagued by a necessary but strong focus on its absolute normative dimension, which makes it difficult to understand research findings when applied to industry examples. There is legitimate support to study normative understandings of a profession where norms are existential: "We wish that journalists would adhere to certain roles and ethical conduct because we think that doing so benefits the larger society" (Reese, 2001, p. 175). Media performances are evaluated in comparison to universal social values such as freedom, equality, fairness, or transparency. This assumption may lead to practical ambiguity, however. For example, how can a normative claim

of transparency involving openness to practices of gathering, organizing, and disseminating information (e.g., Kovach and Rosenstiel,
2001) be explicated to everyday news examples? Multiculturalism as a
professional ideology does not resist in integrating a variety of sources,
issues of representation, or accounting for the number of minorities
working in a newsroom. Most important, Deuze (2006b) argued that
this is looking at "ways in which multiculturalism is given meaning in
the everyday praxis" (p. 390).

Multiculturalism as a Professional Ideology

Multiculturalism requires a constant questioning of how journalistic
sources are presented and how frames are justified. Only by making
visible such implicit structural forces of multicultural frames can journalism students understand how social knowledge is established and
justified by its epistemic relation. It is only in such a way that frames
of other cultures may change and enhance intercultural competence
among media audiences.

Journalists are faced with choices about how to cover cultural conflicts and how to arrive at ethical judgments of what constitutes right
or wrong when covering immigration issues, for example. Such choices
are difficult—"Hard choices between upholding our own cultural
values and considering the values of other cultures" (Ting-Toomey
and Chung, 2005, p. 335). These choices implicitly guide decisions of
whether or not journalists embrace metaethical decision-making processes. Metaethical decisions refer to cultivating choices that transcend
any particular ideological position (i.e., epistemological reflectivity). In
such a process, dealing with ambiguities is part of a maturing inquiry
process. Thinking about multiple consequences of their reporting can
stimulate journalists to "think proactively of the multiple consequences
of each of your choices in assessing an ethical dilemma" (Ting-Toomey
and Chung, 2005, p. 341). Ethical dilemmas can stimulate critical thinking and testing of multiple outcomes and consequences. Such thinking
requires time, which can be probed in the classroom rather than in
the newsroom alone: "Many problematic cultural practices perpetuate themselves because of long-lasting cultural habits or ignorance of
alternative ways of doing things." Hence, reporting the status quo creates less resistance but also less diversity. If new practices of journalists
involve integrating videos that are produced by users, how can such
visual materials be verified? Journalism stands at a juncture, vulnerable
to ongoing structural changes within the journalism profession.

In fact, journalism as an ethical good may be better protected by articulating social and epistemic relations, in which ethical decisions are justified, and by making visible such relations in their practice and in news outputs. That may lead to more engagement with the public, as journalism "is not and never should be disconnected from (the idea of) community—[...] any conceptualization of journalism must always be framed in terms of journalism and society" (Deuze, 2006a, p. 30). Such an idea includes the acceptance of personal biases and the challenge to cope with those, as one US correspondent explained his approach:

> We are all born with some biases, depending on what our backgrounds are and who our parents are, and the idea of being reflective is to understand what these inherent biases are and step back and understand what your point of view might be and then do some reporting that is alternative than what your instinct might be or what your parents might think. The more you do that, the more you are able to understand both sides. In some respect, we are the great generals, we have to be experts, we have to understand what is going on; but we never know everything or can comprehend the situation fully. (personal communication, Washington, DC, January 2012)

6

The Analytical Model of Transnational Journalism Culture

The hardest part is trying to find the truth. They [politicians] always try to manipulate you. For example, they are organizing a press conference, but this does not mean that they try to tell you the truth but that they are trying to bring their political program across the media, to the public. You have to be very, very careful. What you get will be what they want you to get.

—Foreign correspondent, personal communication,
Washington, DC, January 2012

US and foreign correspondents in DC attempt to perform their job (i.e., reporting the truth) guided by their professional ideology (i.e., finding the truth). Performing journalism according to professional ideals is the most challenging part of the journalism profession—and still more challenging for foreign correspondents than for US correspondents. While the news-gathering environment in Washington, DC is structured by transnational principles, the interaction with politicians is still much defined by national borders: politicians guarantee more access to journalists reporting for a national audience than foreign correspondents reporting for an international audience. Globalization has affected the way journalists are connected to sources and has opened new communication networks apart from geographical nation-state borders. Correspondents in DC are working in the capital together but are connected to their home countries through a variety of networks. While the question of access has yielded little change with foreign correspondents still struggling to gain access to important policy makers, the three levels of transnational journalism culture (i.e., the cognitive, performative, and evaluative) explain the need to think differently when conceptualizing news gathering in Washington, DC.

Most importantly, outlining the relationship between correspondents and sources based on the three levels challenges Western normative ideas of source access among correspondents. Access was long believed to be the indicator of success for journalists across the globe (Willnat and Weaver, 2003), but the results showed that access was not the only means to the truth.

This conclusion proposes new ways of thinking about transnational journalism. It first synthesizes disaggregate parts of what is known about journalism culture and then proposes a new framework of transnational journalism cultures. The proposed model of transnational journalism culture is based on the theoretical assumptions of journalism culture (Hanitzsch, 2007a). It explains why it is important to conceptualize the source-correspondent relationship based on those levels that shape a transnational journalism culture.

The Importance of the Three Levels

For the cognitive level, perception and interpretation explain how cultural similarity matters in how correspondents perceive politicians. For the evaluative level, professional roles and ideologies explain how correspondents aim to interact with politicians and which sources they value. Finally, the performative level explains how the performance of correspondents is constrained as well as encouraged by specific news-gathering structures in the capital, such as access rules for US and foreign correspondents. The model presented here outlines the linkage between levels. How do correspondents' perceptions matter for their interaction (i.e., combining the cognitive with the performative level)? How do different truth-telling ideologies manifest in correspondents' sourcing choices (i.e., explaining the performative level with the evaluative level)?

The results represent a rich description of what constitutes the field of journalism in Washington, DC. Furthermore, an investigation of the three levels of journalism culture offers a fresh examination of journalism as a profession using a social-psychological analysis (Donsbach, 2004). The idea of journalists providing value or meaning to a story has long been neglected, particularly in a Western context. However, as this study shows, interpretation and perception (the cognitive element) are important in shaping the interactions of reporters and sources. In essence, intercultural research as well as field theory–based assumptions offered new explanations and an understanding from a viewpoint where it might move journalism practice more into a self-dialogue with its evaluative, performative, and cognitive elements. In essence, the three go together—they define journalism culture, and can be deconstructed for analytical purposes, but in fact represent the same phenomenon (i.e., transnational journalism culture). The book aimed to understand transnational journalism culture at its conceptual level and redefine its dimensional structure based on the reporter-source relationship. Globalization has led journalism scholars to conclude that journalistic orientations and practices are more converged. The proposed model here explains how transnational journalism culture can be made feasible and reveals the complexity of it. Because foreign correspondents still lag in the same amount of access compared to their US counterparts, it may seem that not much has changed on the surface. However, taking into account the network level of analysis and looking at the relationship between correspondents and political sources reveals that journalism performance is deeply structured by the perceptions and interpretations of journalists. The three levels were mapped next to each other by putting the performative level in the middle, as it is the most observable form of transnational journalism culture for the public (because people can directly observe behavior and news reports). The two other levels are less visible but nevertheless powerful in shaping a transnational journalism culture, which eventually shapes the news that journalists produce. The three levels provide the framework of behavior in which journalism is produced. It provides a guideline on how to produce valuable news to an audience. Based on the empirical studies of this book, the model needs to be revised. The book started discussing the three levels of journalism culture. While it makes sense to map those next to each other, the word *level* implies that there is some kind of hierarchy in how the three levels should be conceptualized. Based on the environment of a transnational journalism space, which implies the interactions between people from different countries reporting for various cultural communities, it was assumed that the three levels create distinction in how US and foreign correspondents interact with politicians in the 21st century. The three levels lay out those distinctions that reveal the complexity of studying transnational journalism.

Etic-Emic Approach of Studying Transnational Journalism Culture

The etic approach is interested in the universal and examines common denominators of journalism culture across cultures (Hanitzsch, 2007a). Because the transnational environment is a very specific cultural context, the emic approach further explores the specifics from the viewpoint of DC correspondents. Based on an etic approach, the book analytically identifies the three levels that shape a transnational journalism culture. Hence, while taking an etic approach first helped to analyze how the three levels common in all journalism culture play out in DC, the emic approach explained the very specific cultures of DC correspondents.

Thus, the study tried to understand how journalists' cultural backgrounds (i.e., their field positions) factored into the framing process of sources, based on the analyses of those three levels. Social realities are not described but are instead understood through journalists' work. Such an analysis switches its focus from journalism as what it produces (i.e., news content) toward a sociological analysis of journalists' feel for the game (how news content is produced). Understanding performative, cognitive, and evaluative elements provides new knowledge about how journalists select sources and contributes to journalism theories of why news turns out the way it does. In fact, news as an interpretation of the world can then be understood as existing in a specific time and place tied to a collective habitus (i.e., a history that is part of a news story). Objective structures (i.e., field positions) shape and underpin social life. Through the second stage of the study (the qualitative interviews), an emic approach revealed categories that are important in defining those three levels in a transnational journalism environment. Hence, the emic approach helps illumine the specifics of a transnational context by outlining the categories that are important in shaping the news-gathering environment in Washington, DC. There has been no such a comprehensive study done on combining those two approaches and empirically investigating a transnational journalism space, so doing this contributes to knowledge in journalism studies. In a way, a transnational journalism environment represents a very unique case and thus emic categories remained important to redefine the model of transnational journalism culture and to outline the major categories, which define the three levels.

The Hierarchy of the Three Levels

The empirical studies of this book lead to a new conceptualization of transnational journalism. The transnational journalism model takes into account the implied notion of hierarchy in the word *level* and discusses the three levels and their interdependence.

The Performative Level: The first part of the book conceptualized the performative level of a transnational journalism culture. The performative level in a transnational context is mainly constrained by different amounts of access when comparing journalists from various cultural backgrounds. What we find here is that distinctions on the performative level are visible mainly because of the news context those journalists are reporting for. While the State Department is a very important source of information for foreign journalists, it is less so for US correspondents. The interaction with sources in DC is very much defined by the correspondents' audience. The performative level is also the level to be most likely observed by the public and expresses the cognitive and evaluative level of transnational journalism cultures. Most studies focusing on journalistic performance choose to content-analyze news formats and reveal a rich body of literature on framing or agenda setting that refers to the expression of news performance. Through a transnational cultural analyses, it is possible to observe that those interaction patterns are mostly defined by culture-specific variables such as country of origin or the way those journalists were socialized in their home countries. Cultural differences become more visible in a transnational journalism environment because journalists gather news alongside journalists from other countries. In the qualitative interviews, it becomes evident how the evaluative level (the correspondents' ideal of truth justification) is important in shaping those interactions with politicians.

The Cognitive Level: This study showed that perception and interpretation of source information are shaped by the correspondents' cultural background. Cultural similarity plays an important role in how journalists define the credibility of their news sources. For example, the more journalists perceive a source to think like them, share similar values, and express similar attitudes, the more likely that they will perceive those sources as credible. However, the perfomative aspect matters in how those perceptions influence correspondents: Without personal contact, such perceptions are much less important. Higher amount of social presence in personal interviews may contribute to a higher amount of autonomy because journalists are on the ground, and hence their perceptions might be more likely to influence the stories they report as they become experts because of their unique access and thus become a unique channel of information gathering. Perceptions can further influence the way journalists cover a source in their news: perceived goodwill and background homophily are shown to lead to more positive coverage of political sources. Thus, if we peel the layers of the transnational journalism culture model, we can explain why performance and news content may vary depending on the cognitive level of the transnational journalism culture. The analytical model of transnational journalism culture offers the theoretical framework to test explanations of why news content turns out the way it does. Future studies on transnational journalism can connect those findings to less invisible levels that structure performance.

The Evaluative Level: The innermost level is the core level of journalism culture (i.e., the evaluative level) because journalists' profession is based on truth telling (Kovach and Rosenstiel, 2001), and thus, justification of truth may well be reflected in how journalists interact with their sources. This level shapes how correspondents interact with politicians and how such interactions manifest in content. While the evaluative level reveals how journalists justify truth based on their epistemologies, such worldviews and professional ideologies are also the least likely to be observed in their day-to-day jobs. The evaluative level exists on a rather abstract level defining the practice of reporters but does not influence performance, as norms and values can conflict with other organizational values or ideals. Some researchers believe that evaluative elements (such as norms, journalistic roles, or values) are supposed to eventually shape journalists' practices (e.g., Graber 2002; Weaver et al., 2007). The journalism field is a normative-loaded profession that consists of values, norms, and roles that serve to legitimatize and define journalism. In essence, evaluative ideas as the fundamentals of journalism are the tool and skill sets that set journalism apart from other fields and guarantee its autonomy from heteronomous forces. To understand how evaluative elements inform journalistic practice, it is necessary to reconstruct journalism culture after its deconstruction (i.e., to combine evaluative with performative elements). The empirical study sheds light on how the evaluative element contributes to the practice of journalism or vice versa and in what way a cultural dynamic may explain news content in a transnational journalism environment. However, studies that combine the evaluative and performative levels of a journalism culture are very rare. These studies are much needed to understand journalism culture in particular because of a normative assumption that underlines evaluative elements (i.e., that norms and roles should be evident in news outputs).

Journalists in Western countries highly agree with the normative idea that journalistic roles can only be embodied by the absence of any influences that restrict journalists' autonomy. However, the journalistic practice tells another story. For example, the American public has contradictory ideas about the news media, with 80 percent saying that powerful people and organizations often influence news organizations (Pew Research Center, 2011). Such a mismatch between what the profession ought to be and what audiences perceive the profession to perform requires scholars to look at the practice of journalism. The analytical model is conceptualized to set the framework of such future empirical studies. Such empirical studies are indeed important to gain a holistic view of what a journalism culture entails.

If journalism culture is conceptualized on three levels (see figure 6.1), then studying one level paints only a one-sided picture of a journalism culture. Journalists have a feel for the game (Bourdieu, 1984); it is not a matter of knowing theoretically about journalism (e.g., theories students learn at journalism schools about journalism law and ethics, for example), but a form of competence as an acquired practical

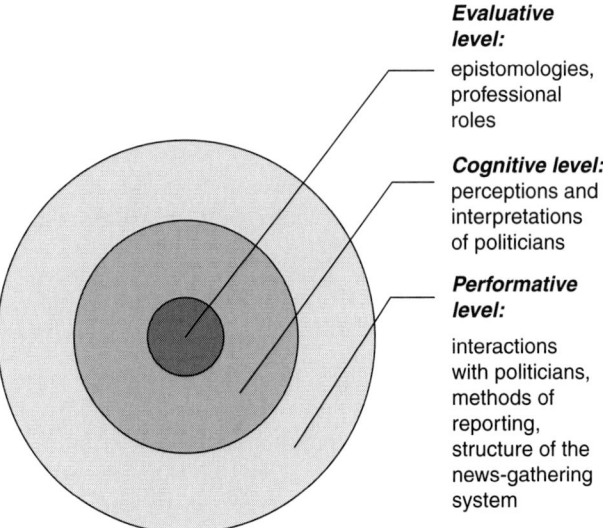

Figure 6.1 Analytical Model of Transnational Journalism Culture.

competence, which is an integral part of Bourdieu's conception of the *habitus*. To achieve a feel for the game, one has to participate in the field in question. A journalist's habitus is formed by learning how to produce news, how to approach a story, how to select sources, how to be different from competitors, and how to play journalism in a specific organization. The feel for the game can differ from one news organization to another. In each case, the structure of the game is internalized in the form of an embodied disposition through practical training. To situate journalists, questions should be posed about this specific *game*. Using this metaphor, the players in the journalism game are sources, coworkers, competitors, audiences, and other interest groups. Sports offer a good example of such a game logic: in a soccer game, every player has a particular function, which structures the game along with rules and other structuring elements (such as duration, halftimes, etc.). However, the outcome of the game is defined by the interaction of these structures (i.e., knowing that France had highly professional players and that the team made it to the final in the 2006 World Cup could not predict the outcome of the World Cup 2010 in South Africa). Players develop a "sense for the game" and a "sense for winning." The knowledge that one of the French star kickers, Zinedane Zidane, is a left-footed player structured the way the other team played and organized their defense. But there is a self-rationality that only plays out in practice. Various interests are involved and the players' positions in the field structure their predisposition toward success. Winning as an outcome of a soccer game explains the logic of a practice of sociology: society offers limited resources to gain symbolic, economic, or cultural capital or pride. But even in limiting situations, "there is no need to appeal to ethical or juridical rules in order to account for practices which are the result of strategies consciously or unconsciously directed towards the satisfaction of a determinate type of material and symbolic interests" (Bourdieu, 1977, p. 47).

A Sense of Journalism

As outlined above, knowing a journalist's or a news organization's position structures the game of journalism, or the *senses of journalism* (e.g., who will be first to publish photos of Britney Spears' baby or who will get the first quote of a newly elected president or prime minister), but this can explain practice only to a certain degree. Throughout the game, journalists develop new senses, and this is why Bourdieu (1977) called a social field a structured structure of practice. An early analysis of the communicator's milieu was spelled out by Darnton (1975) who shared similar arguments with Bourdieu but more specifically in a journalism context. Darnton argued that in order to understand why news turns out the way it does, one has to understand the structure of the reporters' milieu, their newsroom, their relation to primary reference groups (i.e., editors, other reporters, and news sources), their occupational socialization, the way they learn the ropes, and the cultural determinant of their encoding (i.e., standardized techniques of telling stories).

The logic of practice thus includes the play of the game, which is the competition in the newsroom and the hierarchy within it. With specialization and professionalization, journalists have increasingly responded to the influence of their professional peer group as their reference group, which far exceeds that of any images they may have of a general public (Darnton, 1975). The context of work shapes the content of news (i.e., the reinforcement system maintains control over the content). Other scholars have referred to such a journalistic sense or lifestyle as a "journalistic gut feeling" (e.g., Schultz, 2007). Schultz (2007) argued that an important part of media sociology is investigating the seemingly self-evident news values as well as making visible the doxic news values embedded in journalistic practices. In fact, media sociologists have long called for visualizing such "seemingly self-evident" structured structures that play out in practice (e.g., Bourdieu, 1998b; Darnton, 1975; Schultz, 2007).

The Importance of Combining Levels of Journalism Culture

Integrating intercultural communication theories into the field of journalism was challenging. Journalism theories served as cornerstones of this research to account for the field's uniqueness. However, by building on its weaknesses in explaining gaps between normative ideals, practical ideals, and practice, such an analysis sets a framework for looking at practice, delving into theory, envisioning practice in theory, moving back to practice, embracing theory to conceptualize the empirical analysis, and then concluding and interpreting the findings based on correspondents' own reflective statements and paradoxical logics. The strength of this research certainly lies in this dialogue between practice and evaluative component of its practice. This research argues that practices, perception, and norms are integral components of one journalism culture. It is not contrary to the typical assumption that normative theories always move the profession forward because they are principles guiding and defining the field. However, normative theories are only moving the profession forward when becoming practical manifestations, because in their expression (i.e., practice) lies the power and strength of defining the profession and reaffirming its own logic. This is one way of studying change. Practice is controlled by professional ideals and, if that practice puts new pressures on journalists, it is expected to affect their professional ideals. Based on those thoughts, future research implications can be formulated.

Research Implications

Future research can foster an understanding of the interplay between elements of a journalism culture. There are opportunities to study how truth-telling strategies change, how change happens on the normative level when norms are articulated, and how they become manifested in practice by looking at new forms of journalism such as participatory journalists becoming part of the game (i.e., their contribution becoming embedded in traditional news content and thus becoming similar to traditional journalists' output). In such a case, it will be important to base our empirical studies on journalism theory to understand emerging forms of journalism in comparison to earlier forms in order to conceptualize change as the piece in-between. For example, when considering news content from participatory journalists, is there a hierarchy of status recognition of CNN iReporters who offer free-of-charge content to CNN? Are participatory journalists with more cultural and economic capital more likely to be considered for inclusion, as was the case for sourcing practices in traditional media?

Furthermore, as this study shows, scholars should be careful in judging journalists' practices by relying on journalists' responses to normative questions. More valid theories are needed to bridge the gap between role perception and role performance. This is certainly a job that can be achieved by scholarly work in the future and will provide important insights on how journalism is moving from a profession of gatekeepers to a profession based on social relations. One of the largest comparative projects in journalism studies, the Journalistic Role Performance around the World (http://www.journalisticperformance. org), is interested in investigating differences on the performative level (i.e., how journalistic role conceptions manifest in practice). This comparative research project expands the scope of journalism research by including the dimension of news practice into the study of journalism culture. By doing so, the project investigates journalistic role performance cross-nationally and considers the influence that different media systems, organizational constraints, and journalists' role conceptions have on the practice of journalism. Specifically, the study compares journalists' role conceptions with the news stories they produce for each country. Social-system and organizational-level variables further provide an explanatory framework for how to explain this gap. In fact, the project is the first comparative empirical study to investigate the relationship between the evaluative and performative levels of journalism cultures cross-nationally.

On the cognitive level of journalism cultures, more studies are needed to understand how variables such as homophily and source credibility will redefine the profession of journalism as the current society transitions into a digitized networked society. Will such a dynamic change when journalists become more articulated and confident about searching for information online? Will there be a change in the exchange of trust between journalists and audiences when such news-gathering methods become embedded in journalistic routines and naturalized to a higher extent? Social presence and personal contact have been shown to be strong forces of position expression. How will new entrants to the field of journalism transform such expressions of sourcing? Will they be more willing to include participatory voices? Current research shows that journalists who are digital natives and socialized into an online network are significantly more likely to believe that readers' contributions to news content add to truth telling (Hellmueller, Vos, and Poepsel, 2013). How will such battles over normative claims transform the cultural capital of the journalism field? What forces will provoke paradigmatic shifts?

Will a normative battle open up because older journalists might assume that participatory journalists will not adhere to the norms and values of traditional journalists? This situation would certainly transform the hierarchy in the newsroom that has existed for many generations: younger journalists bring with them a skill set that is powerful, and they possess knowledge about the practice, which is no longer solely owned and provided by the older generation of journalists.

Limitations and Concluding Thoughts

This study does come with some important limitations. Foremost, the output of the news organization was measured with self-reported data. Time constraints and access to materials limited the ability to deeply examine what these journalists produced. Nevertheless, another study (Tandoc, Hellmueller, and Vos, 2013), which was a branch of this research, is trying to fill that gap by comparing survey data with content data. There is certainly a need for more such mixed-method designs to capture journalism culture and all its facets. Another important limitation is the response rate. Surveying journalists is a challenge. Surveying a journalist at the political "Broadway" presents another hoop to jump through. As one US correspondent noted: "At the end of last month, I had 30,000 unread emails. I get 300 to 400 e-mails a day" (personal communication, Washington, DC, January 12, 2012).

A bigger sample size would increase the power of this analysis. Regarding the qualitative interviews, a theoretical sampling could not be achieved while gathering the interviews but had to be defined beforehand because of logistical reasons. It was not possible to organize the interviews on a short notice. All of them were arranged about two months ahead because of journalists' tight time schedule and taking into account that those in-depth interviews lasted 55 minutes on average. The qualitative interviews may offer more insights that were not able to be found within the time frame of this research. Furthermore, with every survey comes the price of socially desirable answers. Every attempt was made to ensure the validity and reliability of the survey. Clear distinctions were drawn whether the question explored a normative or a performative level. For example, the "last news story" logic forced correspondents to refer to their practice. However, they are still describing this practice from what they remember. That is where in-depth ethnographical studies are needed to assess the interactions with politicians and capture its unique dynamic from various angles.

This research challenged Western normative ideas. Access was believed to be the indicator of success for journalists across the globe, but the results showed something quite different. More taken-for-granted assumptions in journalism research should be tested under a transnational and multicultural logic. Journalism is moving toward a global logic, but there is greater need of knowledge to explain manifestations or resistances toward such processes by conducting more in-depth studies on the media globalization processes. In addition to media content, future research should investigate what has not been covered to understand the mechanisms of inclusion and exclusion on journalistic quality. This will improve the current understanding of truth-telling claims.

As Bourdieu (1990) has argued in the social sciences, the progress of knowledge presupposes progress in knowledge of the conditions of knowledge. For the journalism profession, the progress of political knowledge in society presupposes progress in knowledge of the conditions of journalistic truth justification based on journalists' position and autonomy in the journalistic field. Such an undertaking may well contribute to an increase of cultural capital in the field and trust among media audiences as it enhances transparency (i.e., disclosure) about the news-gathering process. Considering how trust mechanisms have shifted because of the transparency and openness of the networked environment (e.g., Weinberger, 2009), scholars may need to reconsider trust mechanisms among media audiences based on cultural capital. This requires thinking about the social cement that keeps the journalism profession together. In a digital news environment, media audiences have more potential knowledge about journalists' assessment, journalists' selectivity, and their accuracy of depictions, so trust does not necessarily start with the news organization.

From Weinberger's perspective (2009), journalists choose to practice a passive form of journalism by shifting the responsibility to the public. His argument might lead to the conclusion that if journalists embrace transparency as a new norm, this could increase the credibility of a news organization. However, he does not take into account that transparency cannot stand on its own. It shifts the responsibility from the press to the public, because by being transparent, any reporting is up for discussion. In other words, favoring transparency over objectivity will actually bring us back to the initial problem that the objectivity norm faced: the inexistence of value neutrality. Second, transparency as a method serves its goal only to a certain extent. However, transparency implies that media consumers are actually competent to understanding why and how sources are selected for the news stories. In other words, a transparency norm may serve as a precondition for another norm. But a transparency norm falls short, as journalists' selection process implies, leaving something out because something else is covered. Perhaps, then, values such as care and civic engagement (i.e., Ward, 2009) become more important than objectivity or transparency in understanding what defines journalism.

Hence, studying journalism culture remains an important task. Particularly in a time of change and instability, uncertainty in the profession reminds us that challenges to journalism are challenges to democracy. Besides a high degree of uncertainty inherent in all transactions of different types of capital and their incommensurability, the economic crises, decline of trust in media organizations, and an ongoing globalization promise an even more multilayered paradoxical situation of news gathering. On one hand, the interconnections of social systems force journalists and scholars to think about the global in journalism, whereas national dynamics force journalists to provide a localized discourse to serve local communities. As this study has shown, these connections between the local and the global and its effect on global issues communicated in local settings should be the focus when thinking about a journalism culture. How such contradictory forces are negotiated may vary according to a certain media system. In essence, that may explain why some media organizations have policies in terms of how long foreign correspondents can serve abroad. In a sense, not becoming a US local implies staying *glocal* and acting on a global level but reporting for a local audience—such as the foreign correspondents' audience in their country of origin. It is worth looking at globalization and transnational journalism from all the three levels of journalism culture because, as Reese (2010) stated, "On the institutional surface, perhaps [...] globalization has not yielded much systemic change for journalism. Taking the network level of analysis, however, encompasses the burgeoning connections to media, among media, and among the people involved with them to better account for a life in a globalized world" (p. 352).

Indeed, life in a globalized world involves understanding a global journalism culture as it shapes our knowledge and experiences of the world—from near and far.

Appendix A: Web Survey Instrument and IRB Approval

Survey on Political Journalism in Washington, DC

Campus IRB Approved 5/16/2011

Project Expiration 5/16/2012

Dear Respondent [*insert name of correspondents, first and last name*],

My name is Lea Hellmueller and I am a Doctoral Student from Switzerland, currently working on my dissertation as a Fulbright Visiting Researcher at the Missouri School of Journalism, Columbia.

I would like to ask for your participation in my doctoral research. My dissertation focuses on professional work of Washington correspondents, therefore, your cooperation will determine the success of this study. I am interested in what you have to say about your job and your interactions with politicians. I am specifically interested in your professional experiences you have had and continue to have with politicians as sources in your news work. Thus, your input is very important.

Although participation is voluntary, it is greatly appreciated. Completing this questionnaire should take no more than 15 minutes. There are no known risks to participation in this study. Your participation is completely voluntary and you may end your participation at any time. All of the data gathered in this study will be reported on a group basis and no individual will be identified. Completing this survey certifies that you have read and understand this consent form and agree to be a participant in my dissertation research as described above.

If you have any questions about this study, please feel free to call me (857 869 6380), email me at hellmuellerl@missouri.edu or you can contact my Professor, Dr. Tim P. Vos at vost@missouri.edu. If you have any questions regarding your rights as a research participant, please contact the IRB office at (573) 882 9585.

Thank you very much!

Lea Hellmueller

General instructions: *Please mark your answers with an "x" in the box that best fits your response.*

Confidentiality: All information collected about you and your news organization will be kept on a password-protected database and are strictly confidential. Your name or other information that could be linked to you will not be made available to the public or anyone else in any way. Your name will be deleted from the list and never connected with your answers in any way.

Section 1: Background Information

Q1: Which type of media do you work for? (Please check all that apply):

[ ] Newspaper
[ ] Magazine
[ ] TV station
[ ] Radio station
[ ] Web-based media
[ ] Wire service
[ ] Newsletter
Others, please specify:

Q2: How long have you worked as a journalist (part time and full time)?

[ ] 1 year or less
[ ] More than 1 year, but less than 3 years
[ ] 3 years or more, but less than 5 years
[ ] 5 years or more, but less than 9 years
[ ] 9 years or more

Q3: Have you worked in a profession other than journalism?

[ ] Yes
[ ] No

Q4: What country are you from?

Q5: Can you think of people who inspire you as a journalist? If so, please tell me their names.

Section 2: Political Reporting

For the following questions please reference the most recent interaction or interview with a political source from which at least part of it was aired or published.

Q6: Please briefly summarize the news story.

Q7: Please indicate your feelings regarding his or her function as a politician.

Numbers 1 and 7 indicate a very strong feeling. Numbers 2 and 6 indicate a strong feeling. Numbers 3 and 5 indicate a fairly weak feeling. Number 4 indicates you are undecided.

( ) 1 = Intelligent
( ) 2
( ) 3
( ) 4
( ) 5
( ) 6
( ) 7 = Unintelligent

( ) 1 = Untrained in politics
( ) 2
( ) 3
( ) 4
( ) 5
( ) 6
( ) 7 = Trained in politics

( ) 1 = Cares about the public
( ) 2
( ) 3
( ) 4
( ) 5
( ) 6
( ) 7 = Does not care about the public

( ) 1 = Honest
( ) 2
( ) 3
( ) 4
( ) 5
( ) 6
( ) 7 = Dishonest

( ) 1 = Has others' interests at heart
( ) 2
( ) 3
( ) 4
( ) 5
( ) 6
( ) 7 = Does not have others' interests at heart

( ) 1 = Untrustworthy
( ) 2
( ) 3
( ) 4
( ) 5
( ) 6
( ) 7 = Trustworthy

( ) 1 = Inexpert in his or her field
( ) 2
( ) 3
( ) 4
( ) 5
( ) 6
( ) 7 = Expert in his or her field

( ) 1 = Self-centered
( ) 2
( ) 3
( ) 4

( ) 5
( ) 6
( ) 7 = Not self-centered

( ) 1 = Concerned with the public
( ) 2
( ) 3
( ) 4
( ) 5
( ) 6
( ) 7 = Not concerned with the public

( ) 1 = Honorable
( ) 2
( ) 3
( ) 4
( ) 5
( ) 6
( ) 7 = Dishonorable

( ) 1 = Informed about his or her field
( ) 2
( ) 3
( ) 4
( ) 5
( ) 6
( ) 7 = Uninformed about his or her field

( ) 1 = Moral
( ) 2
( ) 3
( ) 4
( ) 5
( ) 6
( ) 7 = Immoral

( ) 1 = Incompetent in politics
( ) 2
( ) 3
( ) 4
( ) 5
( ) 6
( ) 7 = Competent in politics

( ) 1 = Unethical
( ) 2
( ) 3
( ) 4
( ) 5
( ) 6
( ) 7 = Ethical

( ) 1 = Insensitive
( ) 2
( ) 3
( ) 4
( ) 5
( ) 6
( ) 7 = Sensitive

( ) 1 = Bright
( ) 2
( ) 3
( ) 4
( ) 5
( ) 6
( ) 7 = Stupid

( ) 1 = Phony
( ) 2
( ) 3
( ) 4
( ) 5
( ) 6
( ) 7 = Genuine

( ) 1 = Not understanding
( ) 2
( ) 3
( ) 4
( ) 5
( ) 6
( ) 7 = Understanding

Q7: Please indicate your feelings regarding his or her background.

Table A.1

This political source	Strongly disagree	Disagree	Neutral	Agree	Strongly agree
…is from a social class different from mine	1	2	3	4	5
…does not treat people like I do	1	2	3	4	5
…is from an economic situation like mine	1	2	3	4	5
…shares my values	1	2	3	4	5
…thinks like me	1	2	3	4	5
…and I come from a similar geographic region	1	2	3	4	5
…does not behave like me	1	2	3	4	5
…is different from me	1	2	3	4	5
…treats people like I do	1	2	3	4	5
…has thoughts and ideas that are similar to mine	1	2	3	4	5
…expresses attitudes different from mine	1	2	3	4	5
…has a lot in common with me	1	2	3	4	5
…is from a social class similar to mine	1	2	3	4	5
…is like me	1	2	3	4	5
…does not think like me	1	2	3	4	5
…is similar to me	1	2	3	4	5
…does not share my values	1	2	3	4	5
…behaves like me	1	2	3	4	5
…is unlike me	1	2	3	4	5
…is from an economic situation different from mine	1	2	3	4	5
…does not treat people like I do	1	2	3	4	5
…and I have a similar background	1	2	3	4	5
…is from a social class different from mine	1	2	3	4	5

This political source's	Strongly disagree	Disagree	Neutral	Agree	Strongly agree
…status is different from mine	1	2	3	4	5
…life as a child was similar to mine	1	2	3	4	5
…background is different from mine	1	2	3	4	5
…status is like mine	1	2	3	4	5

Q8: What is your opinion on how much influence each of the following categories had on your last news story (the same news story you referred to above)?

Table A.2

	Strong influence	A great deal of influence	Some influence	Almost no influence	No influence
My own experience with that political source	1	2	3	4	5
Government officials	1	2	3	4	5
News deadline	1	2	3	4	5
My colleagues in my news organization	1	2	3	4	5
My supervisors and higher editors	1	2	3	4	5
My colleagues in other media	1	2	3	4	5
The ownership of my media organization	1	2	3	4	5
Profit expectations of my media organization	1	2	3	4	5
Advertisers	1	2	3	4	5
Feedback from my audience	1	2	3	4	5

Q9: What is your opinion on how much influence each of the following categories *should* have on your day-to-day job?

Table A.3

	Strong influence	A great deal of influence	Some influence	Almost no influence	No influence
My own experience with a political source should have…	1	2	3	4	5
Government officials should have…	1	2	3	4	5
News deadline should have…	1	2	3	4	5
My colleagues in my news organization should have…	1	2	3	4	5
My supervisors and higher editors should have…	1	2	3	4	5
My colleagues in other media should have…	1	2	3	4	5
The ownership of my media organization should have…	1	2	3	4	5
Profit expectations of my media organization should have…	1	2	3	4	5
Advertisers should have……	1	2	3	4	5
Feedback from my audience should have…	1	2	3	4	5

Q9b: On the whole, what do you consider to be the most significant limits on your freedom as a journalist?

Q10: In that specific recent news story, how did your news organization portray this political source?

    ( ) 1 = Unfavorable
    ( ) 2
    ( ) 3

( ) 4
( ) 5
( ) 6
( ) 7 = Favorable

( ) 1 = Negative
( ) 2
( ) 3
( ) 4
( ) 5
( ) 6
( ) 7 = Positive

( ) 1 = Harmful
( ) 2
( ) 3
( ) 4
( ) 5
( ) 6
( ) 7 = Beneficial

( ) 1 = Good
( ) 2
( ) 3
( ) 4
( ) 5
( ) 6
( ) 7 = Bad

( ) 1 = Against
( ) 2
( ) 3
( ) 4
( ) 5
( ) 6
( ) 7 = In favor
( ) 1 = Wise
( ) 2
( ) 3
( ) 4
( ) 5
( ) 6
( ) 7 = Foolish

Q11: Below are statements that relate to news reporting. Please indicate the degree to which each of these statements applies to you. There are no right or wrong answers.

Table A.4

	Scale of Agreement				
	Strongly Disagree	*Disagree*	*Neutral*	*Agree*	*Strongly Agree*
I try to suspend my political preferences when working on news stories.	1	2	3	4	5
I attempt to produce news stories that influence the opinion of my audience.	1	2	3	4	5
It is my job to investigate official claims.	1	2	3	4	5
It is my job to be fair (balanced).	1	2	3	4	5
It is my job to be critical of politicians.	1	2	3	4	5
It is my job to report the news, not become the story.	1	2	3	4	5
It is my job to analyze complex problems.	1	2	3	4	5
Objectivity is a goal that I strive for in my profession.	1	2	3	4	5
It is my job to discuss public policies.	1	2	3	4	5
I attempt to fairly express the position of each side in a political debate.	1	2	3	4	5
It is my job to lay out all relevant sides of an issue in my reporting.	1	2	3	4	5
	Strongly Disagree	*Disagree*	*Neutral*	*Agree*	*Strongly Agree*
It is my job to get information to the public quickly.	1	2	3	4	5
It is my job to convey a positive image of political sources.	1	2	3	4	5
It is important for me not to be perceived as having a political bias in my reporting.	1	2	3	4	5

Continued

Table A.4 Continued

	Strongly Disagree	Disagree	Neutral	Agree	Strongly Agree
My personal feelings should not interfere with reporting the facts.	1	2	3	4	5
I have to provide my audience with the information they need.	1	2	3	4	5
True objectivity in my reporting is impossible.	1	2	3	4	5
I try to maintain a professional distance from my sources.	1	2	3	4	5
My task is to get at the truth.	1	2	3	4	5
I feel I have a moral obligation to report my view as much as to report facts.	1	2	3	4	5
I want to make clear which side in a political dispute has the better-supported position.	1	2	3	4	5
It is my job to be critical of business people.	1	2	3	4	5
It is my job to set the political agenda.	1	2	3	4	5
I attempt to motivate people to participate in civic activity.	1	2	3	4	5
The non-stop news circle does not allow me to double-check my sources.	1	2	3	4	5
It is my job to be impartial.	1	2	3	4	5
Verifying my sources is my first priority.	1	2	3	4	5
My personal feelings should be part of my reporting.	1	2	3	4	5
I attempt to entertain my audience with my stories.	1	2	3	4	5
I am less concerned with my status or reputation than getting the whole story.	1	2	3	4	5
The political affiliation of my audience does not influence my reporting.	1	2	3	4	5
I tell my audience if a political claim is obviously wrong.	1	2	3	4	5
I am concerned how my reporting affects people's political attitudes.	1	2	3	4	5
I want my stories to be interesting for the widest possible audience.	1	2	3	4	5

Q12: After answering question 11, what other beliefs about your professional role as a political journalist influence your daily work? Please write statements that are very important to you as a journalist and which you consider to be your own professional rules.

Section 3: Demographic Information

Q13: What is your gender?

    [ ] Male
    [ ] Female

Q14: Would you say you "grew up using the Internet"?

    [ ] Yes
    [ ] No

THE END—ALMOST:

Q15: Would you like to volunteer for a follow-up interview? If that is the case, please provide your email address so that I can contact you within the next two months. It is very much appreciated.

Q16: Do you have any additional comments about political sources, the survey, or about your work?

_____

THE END – THANK YOU!

Thank you for taking my survey.
Your response is very important to me.

2. WEEK: TUESDAY—Original follow-up letter

SENDING OUT THE ACTUAL SURVEY IN THE MORNING
RE: DISSERTATION RESEARCH STUDY ON CORRESPONDENTS
IN WASHINGTON, DC
SENDING FROM SURVEY GIZMO / HELLMUELLERL@MISSOURI.
EDU

Dear Respondent [*insert name of correspondents, first and last name*],

My name is Lea Hellmueller and I am a Doctoral Student from Switzerland, currently working on my dissertation as a Fulbright Visiting Researcher at the Missouri School of Journalism, Columbia.

I would like to ask for your participation in my doctoral research. My dissertation focuses on professional work of Washington correspondents; therefore, your cooperation will determine the success of this study. I am interested in what you have to say about your job and your interactions with politicians. I am specifically interested in your professional experiences you have had and continue to have with politicians as sources in your news work. Thus, your input is very important.

Although participation is voluntary, it is greatly appreciated. Completing this questionnaire should take no more than 15 minutes. There are no known risks to participation in this study. Your participation is completely voluntary and you may end your participation at any time. All of the data gathered in this study will be reported on a group basis and no individual will be identified. Completing this survey certifies that you have read and understand this consent form and agree to be a participant in my dissertation research described.

If you have any questions about this study, please feel free to call me (857 869 6380), email me at hellmuellerl@missouri.edu or you can contact my Professor Dr. Tim P. Vos at vost@missouri.edu. If you have any questions regarding your rights as a research participant, please contact the IRB office at (573) 882 9585.

Thank you very much!

Lea Hellmueller

General instructions: *Please mark your answers with an "x" in the box that best fits your response.*

Confidentiality: All information collected about you and your news organization will be kept on a password-protected database and are strictly confidential. Your name or other information that could be linked to you will not be made available to the public or anyone else in any way. Your name will be deleted from the list and never connected with your answers in any way.

Day 14: Follow-up mailing—REVISED follow-up letter

RE: DISSERTATION RESEARCH STUDY ON CORRESPONDENTS IN WASHINGTON, DC
SENDING FROM SURVEY GIZMO / HELLMUELLERL@MISSOURI. EDU

Dear Respondent [*insert fist and last name*],

You may recall having received an invitation to participate in my doctoral research study on correspondents in Washington, DC. The study, supported by the Missouri School of Journalism, Columbia, aims at enhancing our knowledge of correspondents and their interactions with politicians in Washington, DC. I'm sending this reminder because you may have not received the invitation, you may have not begun the survey, or you may have only partially completed the survey. Nevertheless, your contribution is very valuable to this research project!

You were selected for this study because of your expertise as a correspondent as you were listed in the Hudson's Media directory or the yellow book (spring 2011). A well-representative sample would be very beneficial for this project. I hope you will devote 15 minutes to complete the questionnaire by next Monday (June 6, 2011). All results will be used for academic purposes only, and as a participant you will receive a full report of the study.

There are no known risks to participation in this study. Your contribution is completely voluntary and you may end your participation at any time or you can skip a question if you choose not to answer. All of the data gathered in this study will be reported on a group basis only (for example: 40% of correspondents working in DC are female/male) and will only be published in academic publications. The questionnaire contains open-ended questions and three measures that are important to have an overall understanding of your work. No individual or news organization will ever be identified. You will never be quoted; your anonymity is guaranteed. Completing this survey certifies that you have read and understand this consent form and agree to be a participant in my dissertation research as described.

If you have any questions about this study, please feel free to call me anytime (857 869 6380), email me at hellmuellerl@missouri.edu or you can contact my Professor Dr. Tim P. Vos at vost@missouri.edu. If you have any questions regarding your rights as a research participant, please contact the University of Missouri IRB office at (573) 882 9585.

Thank you very much!

Lea Hellmueller

General instructions: *Please mark your answers with an "x" in the box that best fits your response.*

Data Privacy Policy

Confidentiality: All information collected about you and your news organization will be kept on a password-protected database and are strictly confidential. Your name or other information that could be linked to you will not be made available to the public or anyone else in any way. Your name will be deleted from the list and never connected with your answers in any way. The software sends out a personal link to every participant to ensure that once you finish the survey, your contact information will be deleted from the list and no reminder will be sent to you. The coding system protects personal information and no individual will ever be identified, because all the data will be reported on a group basis and no media organization or individual will be named.

For administrative reasons, the survey research software needs to limit access only to those selected in the sample, to prevent multiple responses, to follow-up nonrespondents, to compare results over time, or to maintain the responses when an interruption occurs during the web session. The link provided to you includes an identification code and serves as the password for entering the web survey page. You will always have access to your own data collected with the web survey and you will always have the opportunity to modify or even delete it during the data collection process.

The researcher who has access to your data is pledged to protect its confidentiality and is subject to fines if they violate it. Data will only be provided in a form that always protects your identity as an individual.

If you should face any problems with the survey you are more than welcome to let me know. I can also provide you with a Word file to fill out the survey.

Lea C. Hellmueller

Fulbright Researcher
Missouri School of Journalism
246 Walter Williams Hall
Columbia, MO 65211
Phone (cell): (857)-869–6380
Tel: (573) 864–1722
Mail: hellmuellerl@missouri.edu / lea.hellmueller@fulbrightmail.org

PhD student, University of Fribourg, Switzerland

Day 20: Second follow-up mailing—the same letter as follow up 1

RE: DISSERTATION RESEARCH STUDY ON CORRESPONDENTS IN WASHINGTON, DC.
SENDING FROM SURVEY GIZMO / HELLMUELLERL@MISSOURI. EDU

Dear Respondent [*insert fist and last name*],

This is just a quick reminder: You may recall having received an invitation to participate in my doctoral research study on correspondents in Washington, DC. The study, supported by the Missouri School of Journalism, Columbia, aims at enhancing our knowledge of correspondents and their interactions with politicians in Washington, DC. I'm sending this reminder because you may have not received the invitation, you may have not begun the survey, or you may have only partially completed the survey. Nevertheless, your contribution is very valuable to this research project! I hope you will devote 15 minutes to complete the questionnaire.

There are no known risks to participation in this study. Your contribution is completely voluntary and you may end your participation at any time or you can skip a question if you choose not to answer. All of the data gathered in this study will be reported on a group basis only (for example: 40% of correspondents working in DC are female/male) and will only be published in academic publications. The questionnaire contains open-ended questions and three measures which are important to have an overall understanding of your work. No individual or news organization will ever be identified. You will never be quoted; your anonymity is guaranteed. Completing this survey certifies that you have read and understand this consent form and agree to be a participant in my dissertation research as described.

You were selected for this study because of your expertise as a correspondent as you were listed in the Hudson's Media directory or the yellow book (spring 2011). A well-representative sample would be very beneficial for this project. All results will be used for academic purposes only, and as participant you will receive a full report of the study.

If you have any questions about this study, please feel free to call me anytime (857 869 6380), email me at hellmuellerl@missouri.edu or you can contact my Professor Dr. Tim P. Vos at vost@missouri.edu. If you have any questions regarding your rights as a research participant, please contact the University of Missouri IRB office at (573) 882 9585.

Thank you very much!

Lea Hellmueller

General instructions: *Please mark your answers with an "x" in the box that best fits your response.*

Data Privacy Policy

Confidentiality: All information collected about you and your news organization will be kept on a password-protected database and are strictly confidential. Your name or other information that could be linked to you will not be made available to the public or anyone else in any way. Your name will be deleted from the list and never connected with your answers in any way. The software sends out a personal link to every participant to ensure that once you finish the survey, your contact information will be deleted from the list and no reminder will be sent to you. The coding system protects personal information and no individual will ever be identified, because all the data will be reported on a group basis and no media organization or individual will be named.

For administrative reasons, the survey research software needs to limit access only to those selected in the sample, to prevent multiple responses, to follow-up nonrespondents, to compare results over time, or to maintain the responses when an interruption occurs during the web session. The link provided to you includes an identification code and serves as the password for entering the web survey page. You will always have access to your own data collected with the web survey and you will always have the opportunity to modify or even delete it during the data collection process.

The researcher who has access to your data is pledged to protect its confidentiality and is subject to fines if they violate it. Data will only be provided in a form that always protects your identity as an individual.

If you should face any problems with the survey you are more than welcome to let me know. I can also provide you with a Word file to fill out the survey.

Lea C. Hellmueller

Fulbright Researcher
Missouri School of Journalism
246 Walter Williams Hall
Columbia, MO 65211
Phone (cell): (857)-869–6380
Tel: (573) 864–1722
Mail: hellmuellerl@missouri.edu / lea.hellmueller@fulbrightmail.org

PhD Student, University of Fribourg, Switzerland

CALLING SCRIPT for Research Assistant and Lea Hellmueller

(*If they DO NOT ANSWER your call with their NAMES....*)

Hi [*Good morning, good afternoon, good evening—pick one*]
Can I please speak to...... . [*say name from the list, first and last name*]

Hi, I'm [*insert name of research assistant if recruitment is not done by Lea Hellmueller*] a research assistant at the University of Missouri

School of Journalism. I'm calling on behalf of our doctoral student Lea Hellmueller who is conducting a survey with Washington correspondents. You may recall having received a few requests from her in June asking you to participate in her doctoral research study. I'm calling to ask if you'd be willing to participate in the study.

(If they DO ANSWER your call with their NAMES....)

Hi, I'm *[insert name of research assistant if recruitment is not done by Lea Hellmueller]* a research assistant at the University of Missouri School of Journalism. I'm calling on behalf of our doctoral student Lea Hellmueller who is conducting a survey with Washington correspondents. You may recall having received a few requests from her recently asking you to participate in her doctoral research study. I'm calling to ask if you'd be willing to participate in the study.

(If NO)...Sorry to take your time. Have a great day.

(If YES)...That's great, thanks. In that case, I'd like to send you an e-mail link here while we speak *[if it comes up or if they haven't heard about the study, repeat email address]*. If you'd just click on the link, it will take you to the survey. It takes most correspondents 15 minutes or less. Is that okay? The e-mail will come from me, *[insert name of research assistant]* okay? The study is absolutely anonymous. Your link is your password to the study and ensures that everyone can only log on once.

(If MAY BE or if need convincing......)

- The survey is trying to find out how Washington correspondents interact with politicians and is mainly focusing on correspondents' opinion of their work.
- We've gotten a pretty good response so far, but for the study to be valid we need more people to respond. Many people are busy and I don't want to rush or select others for this study, because Lea has carefully selected her potential participants.
- We know you're really busy—that's why we've made the questionnaire as brief as possible. It really does take 15 minutes or less.

(*If it comes up* ...)

- We can't tell you exactly what we're testing or it may bias the results. However, we have gone through the University's Institutional Review Board and they've determined this to be a valuable, scientific study.
- You were selected because of your expertise as a correspondent as you were listed in either the Hudson's media directory or the media yellow book 2011.

(*If they ask* ... Principle investigators:)

- Lea Hellmueller—Fulbright scholar at Missouri school of Journalism and doctoral student. She has been working on this study for the last couple years and your participation is important for her to understand how correspondents work nowadays.
- Tim Vos—he's her advisor at the University of Missouri School of Journalism—he's the author of the book *Gatekeeping Theory* and a number of other studies on journalism and media policy

Instructions:

1. Record one of the following in the spreadsheet:

Enter a "Y" if you reached them and they said yes.
Enter an "N" if you reached them and they said no.
Enter an "M" if you left a voice message and then sent them a link.
If you didn't get a hold of anyone, don't record anything. Just try again another day/time.
→ By the end of the day, report the ones you have reached and agreed to take the survey (to: hellmuellerl@missouri.edu or lea. hellmueller@fulbrightmail.org, so I can follow up with them, if needed)

Copy and paste this message into the email:

Dear [*insert first and last name*],

Thank you so much for agreeing to be part in Lea's doctoral research. She couldn't conduct this valuable, practical journalism research without you!

The survey is ready for your immediate participation. You can start it here:

[*Insert link from spreadsheet, double check name and link—MUST MATCH*]

If you have any questions upon finishing the survey, you can always reach Lea Hellmueller at hellmuellerl@missouri.edu or lea.hellmueller@fulbrightmail.org

Thanks,

[*insert name of research assistant*]

Data Privacy Policy

All information collected about you and your news organization will be kept on a password-protected database and are strictly confidential. Your name or other information that could be linked to you will not be made available to the public or anyone else in any way. Your name will be deleted from the list and never connected with your answers in any way.

The researcher who has access to your data is pledged to protect its confidentiality and is subject to fines if they violate it. Data will only be provided in a form that always protects your identity as an individual.

If you should face any problems with the survey you are more than welcome to let me know. I can also provide you with a Word file to fill out the survey.

————OR————

Dear [*insert first and last name*],

I left you a phone message today asking you to participate in a University of Missouri doctoral research study of journalists. I know you're busy but I hope you'll take the time to complete the survey today or tomorrow.

The survey is ready for your immediate participation. You can start the survey here:

If you have any questions upon finishing the survey, you can always reach Lea Hellmueller at hellmuellerl@missouri.edu or lea.hellmueller@fulbrightmail.org

Thanks,

[insert name of research assistant]

Data Privacy Policy

All information collected about you and your news organization will be kept on a password-protected database and are strictly confidential. Your name or other information that could be linked to you will not be made available to the public or anyone else in any way. Your name will be deleted from the list and never connected with your answers in any way.

The researcher who has access to your data is pledged to protect its confidentiality and is subject to fines if they violate it. Data will only be provided in a form that always protects your identity as an individual.

If you should face any problems with the survey you are more than welcome to let me know. I can also provide you with a Word file to fill out the survey.

ADDITIONAL INFORMATION

If you have any questions, please feel free to email or call me anytime

hellmuellerl@missouri.edu
lea.hellmueller@fulbrightmail.org
phone (US): 857 869 6380

Appendix B: Semi-Structured Interview Guide

Interview Guide

Initial Questions for US and Foreign Correspondents

Introduction: I am conducting a study of the professional work of US and foreign correspondents in Washington, DC. I would like to learn more about your work as a political reporter and your interactions with political sources.

1. Tell me about your background. What motivated you to work as a political correspondent in the DC area? (*Education, years of experience, previous work, etc.*)
2. There's a wide discussion of what journalism is and ought to be. In your opinion, what is a "unique" component of journalism that distinguishes your profession from other professions?
   (To what extent has the function of journalism changed?)
3. What are your most important journalistic values when dealing with political sources? How do you apply them in your job? How did you learn about them?
4. Think of one of your best stories in which you covered a politician in DC. Why was it good? From whom did you receive positive feedback?
5. What are your main sources of information?
6. Let's talk about two politicians in DC, whom you consider particularly valuable for your work. Why are they important? (*past experiences, political experiences/competence, trustworthiness*).
7. How do you maintain the relationship and access with these two sources? How did you get introduced to these sources? (*mode of communication: face-to-face, phone, e-mail, events, etc.*)
8. In what ways has the internet / social media / new technologies altered such an interaction?

9. Let's say that you are covering a story that would benefit from one of the sources' opinion or information. What would be your strategy to approach him/her?
10. Let's talk about the other side of the coin: What kinds of sources are not important and why?
11. What forms of relationships with politicians would you personally not support?
12. Who decides how important a news source is? How is the importance of a news source ultimately established?
13. Compared to foreign correspondents [or compared to US correspondents] in the United States, what do you think are your advantages when dealing with US politicians?
14. Do you share information with foreign [or with US] correspondents?
15. There's a lot of discussion these days about how reporters now can sit in their offices and receive more material more quickly than if they went out and did shoe leather reporting. What do you think about that?
16. What are benefits of establishing close relationships with politicians and what are the disadvantages? How do you maintain your integrity as a journalist? How much "structure" do you perceive coming from your news organization?

Thank you very much for your time!

Toward a Theoretical Framework of Collaborative Autonomy in a Journalistic Field

Research Questions

RQ1a: What forms of cultural capital do journalists embody and perceive as objectified and institutionalized?

RQ1b: What differences exist between cultural capitals of US correspondents and foreign correspondents?

RQ2a: What forms of social capital can be identified as valued in the journalistic field?

RQ2b: What differences exist between social capitals of US correspondents and foreign correspondents?

RQ3a: In what ways has the use of the internet and new technologies as communication platforms altered journalists' collaborative autonomy with political sources?

RQ3b: How is collaborative autonomy perceived in different journalistic fields (US vs. foreign)?

RQ4: How does journalists' dependence on sources affect the cultural capital of the field?

RQ5: How does journalists' dependence on other reference groups such as editors and colleagues alter their cultural capital?

Interview Guide

Initial Questions for US and Foreign Correspondents

Introduction: I am conducting a study of the professional work of US and foreign correspondents in Washington, DC. I would like to learn more about your work as a political reporter and your interactions with political sources.

RQ1

1. **Tell me about your background.** What motivated you to work as a political correspondent in the DC area? (*Education, years of experience, previous work, etc.*)

> THEORY: Embodied cultural capital (*habitus, integral part of correspondent, history, cultural history*)
>
> THEORY: Objectified state of cultural capital (*defined in its relationship with embodied form*), materiality?

RQ1

2. There's a wide discussion of what journalism is and ought to be. In your opinion, what is a "unique" component of journalism that distinguishes your profession from other professions?
   (*To what extent has the function of journalism changed?*)

RQ5

3. What are your most important journalistic values when dealing with political sources? How do you apply them in your job? How did you learn about them?

THEORY: Transmission from embodied cultural capital to objectified cultural capital

THEORY: Institutionalized cultural capital: institutional recognition ("collective magic")

RQ5/RQ6/RQI

3. Think of one of your best stories in which you covered a politician in DC. Why was it good? From whom did you receive positive feedback?

RQ2a/RQ2b

4. What are your main sources of information?
5. Let's talk about two politicians in DC, whom you consider particularly valuable for your work. Why are they important? (*past experiences, political experiences/competence, trustworthiness*)
6. How do you maintain the relationship and access with these two sources? How did you get introduced to these sources? (*mode of communication: face-to-face, phone, email, events, etc.*)

THEORY: Institutionalized social capital

RQ3a

7. In what ways has the internet / social media / new technologies altered such an interaction?
8. Let's say that you are covering a story that would benefit from one of the sources' opinion or information. What would be your strategy to approach him/her?

THEORY: Social Capital in practice

RQ2a/RQ2b/RQ3b

9. Let's talk about the other side of the coin: What kinds of sources are not important and why?
10. What forms of relationships with politicians would you personally not support?
11. Who decides how important a news source is? How is the importance of a news source ultimately established?

> THEORY: Limitations that define the journalistic field

RQ2b/RQ3b

12. Compared to foreign correspondents [or compared to US correspondents] in the United States, what do you think are your advantages when dealing with US politicians?
13. Do you share information with foreign [or with US] correspondents?

> THEORY: Differentiation theory—social capital as resources derived through similarity

14. There's a lot of discussion these days about how reporters now can sit in their offices and receive more material more quickly than if they went out and did shoe leather reporting. What do you think about that?
15. What are benefits of establishing close relationships with politicians and what are the disadvantages? How do you maintain your integrity as a journalist? How much "structure" do you perceive coming from your news organization?

> THEORY: Conversion rates between cultural, social, and economic capital

16. What kinds of challenges and opportunities do you face when dealing with politicians?

References

Allen, J. L., and D. J. Post. (2004). "Source Valence in Assessing Candidate Image in a Local Election." *Communication Research Reports* 21(2), 174–187.

Arnett, C. E., H. H. Davidson, and H. N. Lewis. (1931). "Prestige as a Factor in Attitude Change." *Sociology and Social Research* 16, 49–55.

Baker, C. E. (2002). *Media, Markets, and Democracy.* Cambridge: Cambridge University Press.

Bass, A. Z. (1969). "Redefining the Gatekeeper Concept: A U.N. Radio Case Study." *Journalism Quarterly* 46, 59–72.

Benson, R. (2004). "Bringing the Sociology of Media Back in." *Political Communication* 21, 275–292.

Benson, R. (2006). "News Media as a 'Journalistic Field': What Bourdieu Adds to New Institutionalism, and Vice Versa." *Political Communication* 23(2), 187–202.

Benson, R., and D. C. Hallin. (2007). "How States, Markets and Globalization Shape the News: The French and U.S. National Press, 1965–97." *European Journal of Communication* 22(1), 27–48.

Benson, R., and E. Neveu. (2005). *Bourdieu and the Journalistic Field.* Malden, MA: Polity.

Bentele, G. (Ed.). (2008). *Objektivität und Glaubwürdigkeit: Medienrealität rekonstruiert* [Objectivity and credibility: Media reality reconstructed]. Wiesbaden, Germany: Verlag für Sozialwissenschaften.

Berkowitz, D. (1987). "TV News Sources and News Channels: A Study in Agenda-Building." *Journalism Quarterly* 64, 508–513.

Bourdieu, P. (1977). *Outline of a Theory of Practice.* Cambridge: Cambridge University Press.

Bourdieu, P. (1979). *La distinction: Critique sociale du jugement* [Distinction: A social critique of judgment]. Paris: Editions de Minuit.

Bourdieu, P. (1984). *Distinction. A Social Critique of the Judgment of Taste.* Cambridge, MA: Harvard University Press.

Bourdieu, P. (1986). "The Forms of Capital." In J. G. Richardson (ed.), *Handbook of Theory and Research for the Sociology of Education* (pp. 241–258). New York: Greenwood Press.

Bourdieu, P. (1989). "Social Space and Symbolic Power." *Sociological Theory* 7(1), 14–25.

Bourdieu, P. (1990). *The Logic of Practice.* Cambridge, UK: Polity Press.

Bourdieu, P. (1998a). *On Television.* New York: New Press.

Bourdieu, P. (1998b). *Practical Reason*. Stanford, CA: Polity Press.

Bruns, A. (2005). *Gatewatching: Collaborative Online News Production*. New York: P. Lang.

Byrne, D. (1971). *The Attraction Paradigm*. New York: Academic Press.

Charmaz, K. (2006). *Constructing Grounded Theory: A Practical Guide through Qualitative Analysis*. Thousand Oaks, CA: Sage.

Chibnall, S. (1977). *Law-and-Order News—an Analysis of Crime Reporting in the British Press*. London: Tavistock.

Christians, C. G. (2004). "The Changing News Paradigm: From Objectivity to Interpretative Sufficiency." In S. H. Iorio (ed.), *Qualitative Research in Journalism: Taking It to the Streets* (pp. 41–58). Mahwah, NJ: Lawrence Erlbaum.

Cronkhite, G., and J. Liska. (1976). "A Critique of Factor Analytic Approaches to the Study of Credibility." *Communication Monographs* 43(2), 91–107.

Crossley, N. (2005). *Key Concepts in Critical Social Theory*. Thousand Oaks, CA: Sage.

Darnton, R. (1975). "Writing News and Telling Stories." *Daedalus* 104(2), 175–194.

de Mooij, M. (2010). *Global Marketing and Advertising: Understanding Cultural Paradoxes* (3rd ed.). Thousand Oaks, CA: Sage.

Deuze, M. (2005). "What Is Journalism? Professional Identity and Ideology of Journalists Reconsidered." *Journalism* 6(4), 442–464.

Deuze, M. (2006a). "Global Journalism Education: A Conceptual Approach." *Journalism Studies* 7(1), 19–34.

Deuze, M. (2006b). "Multicultural Journalism Education in the Netherlands: A Case Study." *Journalism & Mass Communication Educator* 60(4), 390–401.

Donsbach, W. (1987). "Journalismusforschung in der Bundesrepublik: Offene Fragen trotz Forschungsboom" [Journalism research in Germany: research questions still remain]. In J. Wilke (ed.), *Zwischenbilanz der Journalistenausbildung (Schriftenreihe der Deutschen Gesellschaft für Publizistik- und Kommunikationswissenschaft Band 14)* (pp. 105–142). Munich, Germany: Communication Science.

Donsbach, W. (2004). "Psychology of News Decisions: Factors behind Journalists' Professional Behavior." *Journalism* 5(2), 131–157.

Donsbach, W. (2008a). "Journalismusforschung im internationalen Vergleich: Werden die professionellen Kulturen eingeebnet?" [International comparative journalism research: Are professional cultures being considered?] In G. Melischek, J. Seethaler, and J. Wilke (eds.), *Medien & Kommunikationsforschung im Vergleich. Grundlagen, Gegenstandsbereiche, Verfahrensweisen* (pp. 271–289). Wiesbaden, Germany: VS Verlag für Sozialwissenschaften.

Donsbach, W. (2008b). "Journalists' Role Perceptions." In W. Donsbach (ed.), *The International Encyclopedia of Communication* (pp. 2605–2610). Malden, MA: Wiley-Blackwell.

Donsbach, W., and B. Klett. (1993). "Subjective Objectivity: How Journalists in Four Countries Define a Key Term of Their Profession." *International Communication Gazette* 51(1), 53–83.

Elliot, D. (2008). "Essential Shared Values and 21st Century Journalism." In L. Wilkins and C. G. Christians (eds.), *The Handbook of Mass Media Ethics* (pp. 28–39). New York: Routledge.

Esser, F. (1998). "Editorial Structures and Work Principles in British and German Newsrooms." *European Journal of Communication* 13(3), 375–405.

Galtung, J., and M. Ruge. (1965). "The Structure of Foreign News." *Journal of Peace Research* 2, 74–91.

Gans, H. J. (1980). *Deciding What's News: A Study of CBS Evening News, NBC Nightly Weeks, Newsweek, and Time*. New York: Vintage Books.

Gans, H. J. (2003). *Democracy and the News*. New York: Oxford University Press.

Gieber, W. (1956). "Across the Desk: A Study of 16 Telegraph Editors." *Journalism Quarterly* 38(3), 289–297.

Glaser, B. G. (1978). *Theoretical Sensitivity*. Mill Valley, CA: Sociology Press.

Glaser, B. G., and A. L. Strauss. (1967). *The Discovery of Grounded Theory: Strategies for Qualitative Research*. Chicago: Aldine.

Golan, G. J. (2010). "New Perspectives on Media Credibility Research." *American Behavioral Scientist* 54(1), 3–7.

Golding, P., and P. Elliott. (1979). *Making the News*. London: Longman.

Golding, P., H. Sousa, and L. van Zoonen. (2012). "Trust and the Media." *Proceedings of the European Journal of Communication* 27(3), 3–6.

Graber, D. A. (2002). *Mass Media and American Politics* (6th ed.). Washington, DC: CQ Press.

Grey, D. L. (1966). "Decision Making by a Reporter Under Deadline Pressure." *Journalism Quarterly* 42, 419–428.

Gudykunst, W. B. (1985a). "An Exploratory Comparison of Close Intracultural and Intercultural Friendships." *Communication Quarterly* 33(4), 270–283.

Gudykunst, W. B., and Y. Y. Kim. (2003). *Communicating with Strangers: An Approach to Intercultural Communication* (4th ed.). New York: McGraw-Hill.

Hage, J. (2004). Foreword. In P. J. Shoemaker, J. W. Tankard, and D. L. Lasorsa (eds.), *How to Build Social Science Theories* (pp. xiii–xvi). Thousand Oaks, CA: Sage.

Hall, S. (1997). *Representation: Cultural Representations and Signifying Practices*. Thousand Oaks, CA: Sage.

Hallin, D. C., and P. Mancini. (2004). *Comparing Media Systems: Three Models of Media and Politics*. New York: Cambridge University Press.

Hanitzsch, T. (2007a). "Deconstructing Journalism Culture: Toward a Universal Theory." *Communication Theory* 17(4), 367–385.

Hanitzsch, T. (2007b). "Die Struktur des journalistischen Felds" [The structure of the journalism fields]. In K.-D. Altmeppen, T. Hanitzsch, and C. Schlueter (eds.), *Journalismustheorie: Next Generation. Soziologische Grundlagen und theoretische Innovation* (pp. 93–105). Wiesbaden, Germany: VS Verlag fuer Sozialwissenschaften.

Hanitzsch, T. (2011). "Populist Disseminators, Detached Watchdogs, Critical Change Agents and Opportunist Facilitators: Professional Milieus, the Journalistic Field and Autonomy in 18 Countries." *International Communication Gazette* 73(6), 477–494.

Hanitzsch, T., K. -D. Altmeppen, and C. Schlueter. (2007). "Zur Einfuehrung: Die Journalismustheorie und das Treffen der Generationen" [Introduction: Journalism theory and the meeting of the generations]. In K.-D. Altmeppen, T. Hanitzsch, and C. Schlueter (eds.), *Journalismustheorie: Next generation. Soziologische Grundlegung und theoretische Innovation.* Wiesbaden, Germany: VS Verlag fuer Sozialwissenschaften.

Hanitzsch, T., F. Hanusch, C. Mellado, M. Anikina, R. Berganza, I. Cangoz et al. (2011). "Mapping Journalism Cultures across Nations: A Comparative Study of 18 Countries." *Journalism Studies* 12(3), 273–293.

Hanitzsch, T., and C. Mellado. (2011). "What Shapes the News around the World? How Journalists in Eighteen Countries Perceive Influences on Their Work." *The International Journal of Press/Politics* 16, 404–426.

Hellmueller, L. (2012). *Disillusioned Working Abroad? U.S. and Foreign Correspondents' Illusio of Professional Freedom.* Paper presented at the International Communication Association Conference, Phoenix, AZ.

Hellmueller, L., T. P. Vos, and M. A. Poepsel. (2013). "Shifting Journalistic Capital? Transparency and Objectivity in the 21st Century." *Journalism Studies* 14(3), 287–304.

Herman, E. S., and N. Chomsky. (2002). *Manufacturing Consent: The Political Economy of the Mass Media.* New York: Pantheon Books.

Hickson, M., III, S. R. Hill Jr., and L. Powell. (1979). "The Foundations of Perceived Similarity." *Communicator* 9(1), 43–51.

Ho, S. S., and D. M. McLeod. (2008). "Social-Psychological Influences on Opinion Expression in Face-to-Face and Computer-Mediated Communication." *Communication Research* 35(2), 190–207.

Holcomb, J., K. Gross, and A. Mitchell. (2011). *How Mainstream Media Outlets Use Twitter: Content Analysis Shows an Evolving Relationship.* Retrieved May 25, 2012, from http://www.journalism.org/analysis_report /how_mainstream_media_outlets_use_twitter?src=prc-headline.

Hovland, C. I., I. L. Janis, and H. Kelley. (1959). *Communication and Persuasion. Psychological Studies of Opinion Change* (3rd ed.). New Haven, CT: Yale University Press.

Hovland, C. I., and W. Weiss. (1951). "The Influence of Source Credibility on Communication Effectiveness." *Public Opinion Quarterly* 15(4), 635–650.

Iyengar, S. (1991). *Is Anyone Responsible? How Television Frames Political Issues.* Chicago: University of Chicago Press.

Johnstone, J. W. C., E. J. Slawski, and W. W. Bowman. (1972). "The Professional Values of American Newsmen." *Public Opinion Quarterly* 36(4), 522–540.

Josephi, B. (2005). "Journalism in the Global Age: Between Normative and Empirical." *Gazette* 67(6), 575–590.

Karlsson, M. (2010). "Rituals of Transparency." *Journalism Studies* 11(4), 535–545.

Kawamoto, K. (2003). *Digital Journalism: Emerging Media and the Changing Horizons of Journalism.* Lanham, MD: Rowman & Littlefield.

Keel, G. (2011). "Journalisten in der Schweiz: Eine Berufsfeldstudie im Zeitverlauf" [Journalists in Switzerland: Chronological study of professional attitudes] In W. Hoemberg, H. Puerer, and R. Blum (eds.), *Forschungsfeld Kommunikation. Band 31.* Konstanz, Germany: UVK Verlagsgesellschaft mbH.

King, S. W. (1976). "Reconstructing the Concept of Source Perceptions: Toward a Paradigm of Source Appropriateness." *Western Speech Communication* 40(4), 216–225.

Kohring, M., and J. Matthes. (2007). "Trust in News Media." *Communication Research* 34(2), 231–252.

Kovach, B., and T. Rosenstiel. (2001). *The Elements of Journalism*. New York: Three Rivers Press.

Kuhn, T. S. (1970). *The Structure of Scientific Revolutions* (2nd ed.). Chicago: University of Chicago Press.

Kunczik, M., and A. Zipfel. (2001). *Publizistik* [Journalism]. Köln, Germany: Böhlau.

Lewin, K. (1947). "Frontiers in Group Dynamics: II. Channels of Group Life; Social Planning and Action Research." *Human Relations* 1(2), 143–153.

Lewis, S. C. (2010). *Journalism Innovation and the Ethic of Participation: A Case Study of the Knight Foundation and Its News Challenge*. Doctoral dissertation, University of Texas at Austin.

Lewis, S. C., K. Kaufhold, and D. L. Lasorsa. (2010). "Thinking about Citizen Journalism." *Journalism Practice* 4(2), 163–179.

Lippmann, W. (1999). Birthday address to the National Press Club. *Nieman Reports* 53/54, 24.

Logan, R. A., and R. L. Kerns. (1985). "Evolving Mass and News Media Concepts: A Q-Study of Caribbean Communicators." *Mass Communication Review* 12(1), 2–10.

Logue, C. M., and E. F. Miller. (1995). "Rhetorical Status: A Study of Its Origins, Functions, and Consequences." *Quarterly Journal of Speech* 81(1), 20–47.

Marr, M., V. Wyss, R. Blum, and H. Bonfadelli. (2001). *Journalisten in der Schweiz. Eigenschaften, Einstellungen, Einflüsse* (vol. 13) [Journalists in Switzerland: characteristics, attitudes, influences]. Konstanz, Germany: UVK Medien.

Mars, L. (2009). *Hudson's Washington News Media Contacts Directory: 2010*. New York: Grey House.

Maton, K. (2003). "Reflexivity, Relationism, and Research: Pierre Bourdieu and the Epistemic Conditions of Social Science Knowledge." *Space and Culture* 6(1), 52–65.

Maton, K., and R. Moore. (Eds.). (2010). *Social Realism, Knowledge and the Sociology of Education: Coalitions of the Mind*. London: Continuum.

McCroskey, J. C., and V. P. Richmond. (1996). *Fundamentals of Human Communication: An Interpersonal Perspective*. Prospect Heights, IL: Waveland.

McCroskey, J. C., V. P. Richmond, and J. A. Daly. (1975). "The Development of a Measure of Perceived Homophily in Interpersonal Communication." *Human Communication Research* 1, 323–331.

McCroskey, J. C., and J. J. Teven. (1999). "Goodwill: A Re-Examination of the Construct and Its Measurement." *Communication Monographs* 66(1), 90–103.

McCroskey, J. C., and T. J. Young. (1979). "The Use and Abuse of Factor Analysis in Communication Research." *Human Communication Research* 5, 375–382.

McCroskey, L. L. (2002). "Domestic and International College Instructors: An Examination of Perceived Differences and Their Correlates." *Journal of Intercultural Communication Research* 31(2), 63–81.

McCroskey, L. L. (2003). "Relationships of Instructional Communication Styles of Domestic and Foreign Instructors with Instructional Outcomes." *Journal of Intercultural Communication Research* 32(2), 75–96.

McCroskey, L. L., J. C. McCroskey, and V. P. Richmond. (2006). "Analysis and Improvement of the Measurement of Interpersonal Attraction and Homophily." *Communication Quarterly* 54(1), 1–31.

McQuail, D., and S. Windhal. (1993). *Communication Models*. London: Longman.

Memoli, M. A., and K. Hennessey. (2012, July 24). "Obama, Romney Campaigns Briefly Touch on Foreign Policy." *The Los Angeles Times*, A6.

Metzger, M. J., A. J. Flanagin, K. Eyal, D. R. Lemus, and R. M. McCann. (2003). "Credibility for the 21st Century: Integrating Perspectives on Source, Message, and Media Credibility in the Contemporary Media Environment." In P. J. Kalbfleisch (ed.), *Communication Yearbook* 27 (pp. 293–335). Mahwah, NJ: Lawrence Erlbaum.

Neuliep, J. W. (2003). *Intercultural Communication: A Contextual Approach* (2nd ed.). Boston: Houghton Mifflin..

Neuliep, J. W., S. Hintz, and J. C. McCroskey. (2005). "The Influence of Ethnocentrism in Organizational Contexts: Perceptions of Interviewee and Managerial Attractiveness, Credibility, and Effectiveness." *Communication Quarterly* 53(1), 41–56.

Olmstead, K., A. Mitchell, and T. Rosenstiel. (2011). *The State of the News Media*. Retrieved February 15, 2012, from http://stateofthemedia.org/2011/online -essay/.

Patterson, T. E., and W. Donsbach. (1996). "News Decisions: Journalists as Partisan Actors." *Political Communication* 13(4), 455–468.

Perry, E. L. (2006). *Infusing the Curriculum: Making Cross-Cultural Journalism a Requirement of the Next Generation*. Paper presented at "Rethinking the Discourse on Race: A Symposium on How the Lack of Racial Diversity in the Media Affects Social Justice and Policy," St. John's University School of Law, Queens, New York, April 28–29.

Peterson, S. (1979). "Foreign News Gatekeepers and Criteria of Newsworthiness." *Journalism Quarterly* 56, 116–125.

Pew Research Center. (2011). *Press Widely Criticized, but Trusted More Than Other Sources of Information*. Retrieved March 3, 2012, from http://pewre search.org/pubs/2104/news-organizations-inaccurate-trust-cable-news-press -media-coverage.

Pew Research Center's Project for Excellence in Journalism (2009). *The New Washington Press Corps*. Retrieved July 17, 2012, from http://www.journalism .org/analysis_report/new_washington_press_corps.

Plano Clark, V. L., and J. W. Creswell. (2008). *The Mixed Methods Reader*. Thousand Oaks, CA: Sage.

Powers, A., and F. Fico. (1994). "Influences on Use of Sources at Large U.S. Newspapers." *Newspaper Research Journal* 15(4), 87–97.

Prosser, M. H. (1978). *The Cultural Dialogue: An Introduction to Intercultural Communication.* Boston: Houghton Mifflin.

Quandt, T., M. Löffelholz, D. H. Weaver, T. Hanitzsch, and K. -D. Altmeppen. (2006). "American and German Journalists at the Beginning of the 21st Century." *Journalism Studies* 7(2), 171–186.

Reese, S. D. (1990). "The News Paradigm and the Ideology of Objectivity: A Socialist at the Wall Street Journal." *Critical Studies in Mass Communication* 7(4), 390–409.

Reese, S. D. (2001). "Understanding the Global Journalist: A Hierarchy-of-Influences Approach." *Journalism Studies* 2(2), 173–187.

Reese, S. D. (2008). "Theorizing a Globalized Journalism." In M. Loeffelholz and D. Weaver (eds), *Global Journalism Research: Theories, Methods, Findings, Future.* London: Blackwell.

Reese, S. D. (2010). "Journalism and Globalization." *Sociology Compass* 4(6), 344–353.

Reese, S. D., and J. Ballinger. (2001). "The Roots of a Sociology of News: Remembering Mr. Gates and Social Control in the Newsroom." *Journalism & Mass Communication Quarterly* 78(4), 641–658.

Reese, S. D., and S. C. Lewis. (2009). "Framing the War on Terror: The Internalization of Policy in the U.S. Press." *Journalism* 10(6), 777–797.

Roper, B. W. (1985). *Public Attitudes toward Television and Other Media in a Time of Change.* New York: Television Information Office.

Rosten, L. C. (1937). "President Roosevelt and the Washington Correspondents." *Public Opinion Quarterly* 1(1), 36–52.

Rothman, S., and S. R. Lichter. (1985). "Personality, Ideology and World View: A Comparison of Media and Business Elites." *British Journal of Political Science* 15(1), 29–49.

Sattler, W. M. (1947). "Conception of Ethos in Ancient Rhetoric." *Speech Monographs* 14(1), 55–65.

Schotz, A. (2008). "Source Credibility Is Part of Our Duty." *Quill* 96(8), 30–30.

Shoemaker, P. J. (1984). "Political Group Viability as Predictor of Media Attitudes." *Journalism Quarterly* 61(4), 889–892.

Shoemaker, P. J. (1991). *Communication Concepts: Gatekeeping* (vol. 3). Newbury Park, CA: Sage.

Shoemaker, P. J. (1993). "Critical Thinking for Mass Communications Students." *Critical Studies in Mass Communication* 10(1), 99–112.

Shoemaker, P. J., and S. D. Reese. (1991). *Mediating the Message.* White Plains, NY: Longman.

Shoemaker, P. J., and S. D. Reese. (1996). *Mediating the Message: Theories of Influences on Mass Media Content* (2nd ed.). White Plains, NY: Longman.

Shoemaker, P. J., J. W. Tankard, and D. L. Lasorsa. (2004). *How to Build Social Science Theories.* Thousand Oaks, CA: Sage.

Shoemaker, P. J., and T. P. Vos. (2009). *Gatekeeping Theory.* New York: Routledge.

Singer, J. B. (2005). "The Political J-Blogger: 'Normalizing' a New Media Form to Fit Old Norms and Practices." *Journalism* 6(2), 173–198.

Singer, J. B. (2007). "Contested Autonomy: Professional and Popular Claims in Journalistic Norms." *Journalism Studies* 8(1), 79–95.

Singer, J. B. (2010). "Norms and the Network: Journalistic Ethics in a Shared Media Space." In C. Meyers (ed.), *Journalism Ethics: A Philosophical Approach* (pp. 117–129). New York: Oxford University Press.

Slater, S., and H. Jones. (2012). *Bank Rate Rigging Scandal Widens: Diamond Fights on*. Retrieved August 22, 2012, from Reuters News: http://www.reuters.com/article/2012/06/29/us-libor-banks-idUSBRE85S0P420120629.

Starck, K., and J. Soloski. (1977). "Effect of Reporter Predisposition in Covering Controversial Story." *Journalism Quarterly* 54(1), 120–125.

Strömbäck, J., and D. V. Dimitrova. (2006). "Political and Media Systems Matter: A Comparison of Election News Coverage in Sweden and the United States." *Harvard International Journal of Press/Politics* 11(4), 131–147.

Tandoc, E., L. Hellmueller, and T. P. Vos. (2013). "Mind the Gap: Between Journalistic Role Conception and Role Enactment." *Journalism Practice* 7(5), 539–554.

Terkel, A. (2012, July 17). *Sherrod Brown Hugging His Wife in Photo Prompts Conservative Bloggers Conspiracy Theory*. The Huffington Post. Retrieved July 18, 2012, from http://www.huffingtonpost.com/2012/07/17/sherrod-brown-wife-blogger_n_1681169.html.

Teven, J. J. (2008). "An Examination of Perceived Credibility of the 2008 Presidential Candidates: Relationships with Believability, Likeability, and Deceptiveness." *Human Communication* 11(4), 391–407.

Ting-Toomey, S., and L. C. Chung. (2005). *Understanding Intercultural Communication*. Los Angeles, CA: Roxbury Publishing.

Tresch, A. (2009). "Politicians in the Media: Determinants of Legislators' Presence and Prominence in Swiss Newspapers." *International Journal of Press/Politics* 14(1), 67–90.

Tuchman, G. (1978). *Making News: A Study in the Construction of Reality*. New York: Free Press.

U.S. Department of State. (2012). *Ground Rules for Interviewing State Department Officials*. Retrieved May 16, 2012, from http://www.state.gov/r/pa/prs/17191.htm.

Wahl-Jorgensen, K., and T. Hanitzsch. (2009). *The Handbook of Journalism Studies*. New York: Routledge.

Waisbord, S. (2004). McTV: "Understanding the Global Popularity of Television Formats." *Television & New Media* 5(4), 359–383.

Ward, S. J. A. (2009). "Truth and Objectivity." In L. Wilkins and C. G. Christians (eds.), *The Handbook of Mass Media Ethics* (pp. 71–83). New York: Routledge.

Weaver, D. H., R. A. Beam, B. J. Brownlee, P. S. Voakes, and G. C. Wilhoit. (2007). *The American Journalist in the 21st Century: U.S. News People at the Dawn of a New Millennium*. Mahwah, NJ: Lawrence Erlbaum.

Weaver, D. H., and G. C. Wilhoit. (1986). *The American Journalist: A Portrait of U.S. News People and Their Work*. Bloomington: Indiana University Press.

Weaver, D. H., and G. C. Wilhoit. (1996). *The American Journalist in the 1990s: U.S. News People at the End of an Era*. Mahwah, NJ: Lawrence Erlbaum.

Weinberger, D. (2009). *Transparency Is the New Objectivity*. Retrieved August 1, 2012, from http://www.hyperorg.com/blogger/2009/07/19/transparency-is-the-new-objectivity/.

Weischenberg, S. (1995). *Journalistik. Theorie und Praxis aktueller Medienkommunikation. Band 2: Medientechnik, Medienfunktionen, Medienakteuere: Theorie und Praxis aktueller Kommunikation* [Journalism theory and praxis current media communication (vol. 2): media technology, media function, media actors: theory and praxis current communication]. Wiesbaden, Germany: VS Verlag für Sozialwissenschaften.

Weischenberg, S., M. Malik, and A. Scholl. (2006). Journalismus in Deutschland [Journalism in Germany]. *Media Perspektiven* 7, 346–361.

Westley, B. H., and M. S. MacLean. (1957). "A Conceptual Model for Communications Research." *Educational Technology Research and Development* 3(1), 31–38.

White, D. M. (1950). "The Gatekeeper: A Case Study in the Selection of News." *Journalism Quarterly* 27, 383–396.

Wiley, S. (2004). "Rethinking Nationality in the Context of Globalization." *Communication Theory* 14(1), 78–96.

Willnat, L., and D. H. Weaver. (2003). "Through Their Eyes: The Work of Foreign Correspondents in the United States." *Journalism* 4(4), 403–422.

Worlds of Journalisms Project. (2007). *Master Questionnaire: Journalists.* Retrieved August 1, 2012, from http://www.worldsofjournalism.org/docs/Master%20questionnaire%20journalists%20EN%20final.pdf.

Wright, K. B. (2000). "Perceptions of Online Support Providers: An Examination of Perceived Homophily, Source Credibility, Communication and Social Support within Online Support Groups." *Communication Quarterly* 48, 44–59.

Yoon, Y. (2005). "Examining Journalists' Perceptions and News Coverage of Stem Cell and Cloning Organizations." *Journalism & Mass Communication Quarterly* 82(2), 281–300.

Yoos, G. E. (1979). "A Revision of the Concept of Ethical Appeal." *Philosophy & Rhetoric* 12(1), 41–58.

Index

Printed and bound in Great Britain by
CPI Group (UK) Ltd, Croydon, CR0 4YY